I'M NOT DEAD YET

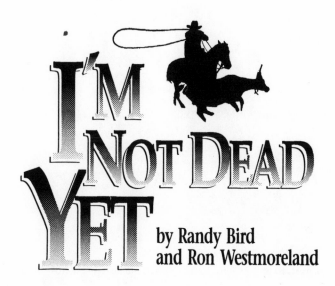

I'M NOT DEAD YET

by Randy Bird
and Ron Westmoreland

WRS
PUBLISHING

A Division of WRS Group, Inc.
Waco, Texas

First published in the United States of America in 1992 by WRS Publishing,
A Division of WRS Group, Inc., 701 N. New Road, Waco, Texas 76710
Design by Kenneth Turbeville

Library of Congress Cataloging-in-Publication Data

Bird, Randy, 1954–
    I'm not dead yet / by Randy Bird and Ron Westmoreland.
        p.   cm.
    ISBN 1-56796-000-6 : $19.95
    1. Bird, Randy, 1954–   . 2. Cowboys—United
States—Biography. 3. Paraplegics—United States—Biography.
I. Westmoreland, Ronald P., 1934–   . II. Title.
GV1833.6.B57A3 1993
636.2'0'092—dc20
    [B]   92-33272
                                                            CIP

To all my family and friends. Without their help,
I would not have made it through the last six years.

Table Of Contents

Acknowledgments

Randy Bird: I'd like to thank Pa, Edgar Barefield, for all of his support and understanding; Nanny, Elgie Barefield, for all her prayers and good cooking; my mother, Betty, who stayed by my side every night; my wife, Marilyn, for putting up with me; Brett, for being there, and for being willing to do anything Daddy asked him to do; Christina, just for being pretty; Matthew, for being a mess; my father, James (Jim), for teaching me to be a winner; my sister, Peggy Sue, for being supportive; James, for making the decision that, no matter what, he was willing to do whatever I needed; and Papa Bill (Bill Watson), for understanding that Mother had to be away for so long. I especially want to thank Ron—there is no way I could have told my story or put it down on paper without him.

Ron Westmoreland: I'm grateful to hospital and emergency personnel and to Randy's friends and family for their input. Without them, the story would not be complete. I thank Terri Johnson and Margaret Leary for being kind in their editorial comments. Most of all, I thank my wife, Betty Ann, who was with me through the long days and nights, offering encouragement and advice.

Foreword

I've been a cowboy for most of my life, so I can understand why Randy Bird would want to return to riding horses after his disabling accident. In fact, in our love for horses and the cowboy way of life, Randy and I have much in common. So it's easy for me to see why Randy couldn't wait to get back on his horse after the accident that damaged his spinal cord. However, the amount of pain and struggle involved in Randy's return to riding is quite extraordinary.

Even when playing the hero in numerous movies, I seldom encountered a story of such courage and tenacity.

People all over the world—those who have been severely injured in accidents as well as those simply struggling to live a good life—will take new heart when they read this book. Chills will run down their spine as they live with Randy through the immense pain of the weeks and months following his accident. The way Randy fought back when the doctors had given him up for dead will breathe new zest into those who find life a struggle for whatever reason.

Randy's grandfather, Pa, used to sum it all up pretty well when he would tell the young Randy that, no matter what the circumstances, there is always hope. That became Randy's slogan when the accident robbed him of his mobility and the temptation to give up was overpowering. And those words, Pa's continual encouragement, and the love of all Randy's family and friends, were vital to sustaining his will to live and fight for a future.

Faith in God—something else Randy and I share—was the basis upon which Randy built his fight back to health and a happy and productive life. Without the sense that God was watching over him—had indeed spoken to him shortly after his truck flipped over—Randy may not have been able to endure the medical procedures, the setback from his stroke, the constant infections, and his inability to walk.

Nor would he have the experience from which to draw as he talks with children and adults all over the country, giving hope where none exists.

Randy often asks himself, "What else does life have in store for this ol' cowboy?" While he doesn't yet know the answer to that question, he's busy preparing for the future. Already he's designed and built a special saddle—one that enables himself and other disabled people to ride without the benefit of stomach muscles and a healthy spine. And he produces these saddles himself—each one designed to accommodate the buyer's particular challenges. His hope is that being able to ride a horse without help from someone else will give many people with disabilities the chance of riding tall in the saddle, of experiencing dignity and independence. (He also builds saddles for those without physical disabilities.)

He's visited rehabilitation centers and hospitals, schools and churches in an effort to spread his philosophy: that disabled people should not settle for being limited by other people's expectations; they must simply find different ways of doing things.

There's no doubt in my mind that Randy is well on the way to making his own happy trails.

—Roy Rogers

Chapter 1

Like most northeast Texas February mornings, the day dawned cold and clear. Smoke billowed from the ranch-house chimney, spreading a pine-scented haze through the surrounding trees.

Randy Bird had just finished hooking up his horse trailer to his new Ford pickup. As he walked briskly to the house for one last cup of coffee before cleaning up Ten, his bay stallion, he rubbed his cold hands together. In a futile attempt to ward off the icy wind, he pulled his black cowboy hat down to where his ears touched the wide brim.

Inside, Gary Mitchell, Randy's rodeo buddy, was standing in front of the potbellied stove, drinking a steaming cup of coffee. Gary and Randy shared living expenses and the high cost of traveling to rodeos.

"Did you drink all the coffee?" Randy asked, as he slammed the door behind him.

"Nope," Gary answered, never looking up.

Randy poured the last of the thick, black brew into his cup and stood as close to the stove as he could without actually touching it.

"Want to go with us today?" Randy asked, as he took a big swallow of coffee.

"Naw, got other things to do."

"All you got is women on your mind," Randy replied.

"Nothin' wrong with that. Beats standing around watching a bunch of guys chasing cows."

"Jerry Jenkins is going. You might as well come too."

"Appreciate it, but I'll see you later on."

They stood silently for several minutes, both lost in their thoughts for the day.

"Well, much as I hate to, I got to catch ol' Ten and clean the ornery little cuss up," Randy said, breaking the silence.

"That horse ought to be in some stock contractor's bucking string rather than cutting cows," Gary commented.

"He's a little snorty, but once you get the buck out of him, he'll flat cut a cow," Randy answered, defending the bay stallion.

Randy went to the kitchen, rinsed out his coffee mug, and headed off toward the barn.

Watch Joe, a sorrel gelding, stuck his head through the open part of the stall door as Randy walked down the barn aisle. The horse was special to Randy and received more attention than all the other horses he owned.

"Hi, Joe," he said, petting Watch Joe on the neck. "Got to get ol' Ten cleaned up and get the show on the road."

He glanced down at the small round scar on the sorrel's chest. The horse was a living miracle. Three years earlier, when he was just a three-month-old colt, he had been shot with a high-powered rifle. The wound had been a gaping hole the size of a man's fist. But Joe was alive and well now, and special to Randy.

Randy grabbed a halter from the tack room and walked to Ten's stall. He stood at the door, admiring the young bay stallion.

Ten had shown well, but had fallen short of winning. He just needed that little extra seasoning. The various jackpot cuttings held near Randy's place would give him the opportunity to gain experience without costly entry fees. He might be a little snorty, but he sure fit what Randy looked for in a good horse. The stallion was bred to cut cows. All he needed was riding and cow work.

Randy opened Ten's stall door and stepped in, talking. "How're you doin' this morning?" he cooed, as he slowly approached the stallion.

The horse snorted loudly and faced Randy with his head high, ears up, nostrils flared.

Randy smiled as he remembered what Gary had said about Ten belonging in a bucking string. He held his hand out and slowly touched the bay on the jaw. The horse immediately jerked his head back, but didn't move his body. Randy eased beside him, put his right arm over the horse's tense neck, slid the halter over his nose, and buckled it.

"Well, fellow, that wasn't so bad, was it?" Randy asked, as he led Ten into the barn hallway.

The bay stallion walked as if on eggshells. His eyes were wide and bright and no movement went unnoticed.

Randy ran the halter lead rope through the steel ring mounted on an aisle post, and tied it in a slipknot. Standing next to Ten, he picked up each foot, scraping it clean with a hoof pick. The bay wasn't overly fond of the procedure, but other than shifting his weight onto Randy, he didn't cause any problems. Randy spent the better part of an hour brushing and grooming the horse until his coat glistened.

Randy backed off and liked what he saw.

"Man, you're a good-lookin' sucker," Randy remarked as he gave the horse a pat on the rump.

He replaced the grooming tools in the tack room and picked up his saddle from the rack.

"Well, ol' boy, think I'll ride you for a few minutes. Maybe that'll take some of the buck out of you before we get over to the arena," Randy said, as he placed the saddle on the bay's back.

The stallion had such a hump in his back that the saddle raised up high enough for Randy to stick his fist between the saddle and the horse's back.

"Oh, oh, looks like it's goin' to be one of those mornings," Randy remarked, as he slipped the bit in the horse's mouth.

He led the stallion out to the sandy arena, careful to close and latch the gate behind him. If Ten managed to buck him off, he didn't want to have to chase him down as well.

Randy stood next to Ten's left shoulder. He held the reins in his left hand and grabbed the saddle horn with his right. He stuck his left foot into the stirrup until his boot heel jammed tight against the hard rawhide. Taking a deep breath, he swung his right leg over the cantle of the saddle and found the right stirrup. The stallion's body became tense and unyielding as Randy settled down into the saddle.

"Well, young man, let's see if you're goin' to be able to buck me off today," Randy said out loud, as he touched the bay with a slick boot heel.

The horse started to walk off, then jumped forward, pulling up the slack in the reins. His head disappeared between his legs, and the ride was on. Randy tightened his grip on the reins and regained his position in the saddle after the initial buck. After three or four bone-jarring leaps, the horse pulled up and blew hard through his flared nostrils. It was all over for the morning. This was an everyday ritual— one that both the stallion and Randy enjoyed.

Randy smiled as he patted Ten on the neck. Then he touched the horse with his heels and the two moved out at a brisk trot.

It was getting close to noon before Randy loaded the horse and headed toward Jerry Jenkins' place. Jerry wasn't taking a horse that day, but planned on watching.

After Randy picked up Jerry, they arrived at Green Acres shortly before 1:00 p.m., giving Randy enough time to warm the horse up and get himself mentally prepared for the cutting contest.

Randy unloaded Ten, tightened the girth, mounted up, and began walking the stallion with the other cutting contestants. By 1:00 p.m. the arena was filled with horses and riders.

Randy glanced from one horse to another, comparing each to his own bay stallion. He smiled, patted Ten's neck and straightened his long mane. "It don't get much better than this," he thought, as he continued to ride around the arena.

Ever since Randy had been a youngster, he had had some kind of horse to ride. His fondest memories involved horses. He had been active in other sports throughout his school years, but horses were his life.

There were several entries in the cutting contest. There were to be three go-'rounds and the entry with the best score overall would be the winner.

Randy watched as each horse performed. Then his name was called over the loudspeaker. He eased the stallion into the cow herd, careful not to excite them. He moved deliberately toward a stout-looking, white-faced yearling that had shown a lot of action earlier. The stallion stepped between the calf and the herd. The white-face wheeled in an attempt to rejoin the herd, but the horse quickly went nose-to-nose with the calf. The calf and horse darted from side to side, but the aggressive stallion blocked all attempts. Too soon, the whistle blew, marking the end of Randy's time. He smoothly pulled up on the reins, letting the stallion know to stop working the calf.

As Randy rode from the arena, a mounted cowboy asked, "What have you been feeding ol' bay? He acted like he wanted to work that cow."

Randy smiled, knowing that was about as much of a compliment as he was going to get. But he knew his horse had done well, and that was all that mattered.

After the scores were counted and double-checked, Randy was declared the winner.

"By golly, it isn't the national championship," Randy thought proudly, "but it does show that he can win."

Butch Green, a team roper from Caddo Mills, shouted at Randy to hold up. Randy waited as Butch walked toward him.

"Can you head for me in the team roping?" Butch asked.

"Don't have anything to head on. Besides, I haven't headed a steer in two or three months," Randy replied.

"That ain't a problem. I can borrow a horse."

"All right. But remember, don't gripe if I miss," Randy said, smiling.

Butch waved and disappeared into the crowd of horses and cowboys, only to return in a few minutes leading a borrowed horse.

Randy adjusted the stirrups and mounted the unfamiliar horse. He borrowed a heading rope from Butch and reminded him again not to complain if he missed.

Randy and Butch waited their turn to rope, then rode into the arena. Randy glanced at Butch to make sure he was ready, then nodded his head to the gateman who would let the steer free.

The gate flew open. Randy touched the horse's side with his heels and the horse leapt from the box. Randy brought his rope up over his head in a twirling motion. One, two, three rounds, then a hard toss toward the horns of the running steer. The loop landed around the base of the steer's horns. In one smooth motion, Randy pulled the rope tight and quickly made two loops around the saddle horn as the horse turned to the left, leading the steer behind him. Butch moved in behind the steer and quickly threw a loop that settled around both hind legs. The ropes tightened and the horses faced each other. The run was complete.

Randy and Butch both knew it was a good performance.

Later, as they prepared to leave, Randy and Butch were named as winners.

It was getting close to dark by the time Randy and Jerry loaded the bay stallion. Randy was pleased with his horse's performance and felt pretty good about the day's events.

"How about going to the Southern Junction for a beer?" Jerry asked.

"Naw, man, I've got to get up early in the morning,"

Randy replied, as they jolted along the rough road.

"Aw, come on, just one beer and maybe a couple of dances."

"OK, but just for a little while. Man, I'm serious, I've got a long day tomorrow."

Randy dropped Jerry off and got home after dark. He unloaded the stallion and put him in his stall. Then he fed him and the other horses. As he unhooked the trailer from the truck, he wished he hadn't told Jerry he would go.

By the time he got cleaned up, picked up Jerry, and drove to Rockwall, it was about 8:00 p.m.

Leaving Rooster, Randy's cowdog, to guard the truck, they walked into the building. The place was already alive, and Randy and Jerry just blended in. The first beer was forgotten about, and one called for another. There was a lot of rodeo and horse talk among the cowboy crowd. And there were ladies to dance with. The night went by quickly and it was 2:00 a.m. before Randy realized the time.

"Come on, Jerry, we got to head toward the house," Randy shouted over the loud band.

The two friends left the building and headed across the parking lot.

Rooster was still lying on top of the toolbox, watching over his master's truck.

"Hey, Rooster, get any shut-eye?" Randy asked, running his hand down the dog's back.

The tired cowboys slowly settled into the pickup's padded seats and Randy waited for the defroster to clear the windows before he backed out the truck.

"Dang, it's cold," Jerry commented, as he crammed his hands into his coat pockets.

"I hear that," Randy replied, as he turned his head to make sure it was clear to back up.

Neither spoke again until Randy pulled up in front of Jerry's house.

"Enjoyed it," Randy yawned.

"Yep, we'll do it again," Jerry replied.

Randy waited until Jerry shut the door, then put the truck into motion.

Chapter 2

The white line in the middle of the farm-to-market road curved left, then right, never seeming to take a straight path. Randy clicked the high beams on as he glanced at the dashboard clock. He sighed as he saw the time. "Man, it's three o'clock in the morning, and I've got to be in Irving at half past six. Wish I'd stayed home," he thought, rubbing his tired eyes.

He could hear Rooster scratching and sliding around on the toolbox mounted behind the cab as the truck swayed back and forth.

"I've got to install carpet on that toolbox before Rooster slides off… should have made him stay home in the first place. Maybe I can carpet it next weekend," he thought.

Randy's mind drifted back to the events of the day. All in all, it had been good. The weather had been decent for a change, and Ten had won the cutting. Maybe it was time to enter him in higher-stake cutting contests. The young stallion would do even better if Randy could spend more time working with him. "But when a fellow has to work for a living, he just does what he can, when he can," thought Randy.

He wished he could get a couple of hours' sleep, but all he

had time for was a quick shower and a hurried drive to Irving.

Without warning, the white line curved sharply to the left. Randy jerked the steering wheel in response and was immediately aware of Rooster's attempt to get some footing on the slick toolbox. Randy momentarily panicked and abruptly cut the steering wheel back to the right to try to keep Rooster from sliding off. Glancing anxiously over his shoulder, Randy realized the dog had somehow managed to stay atop the toolbox.

He quickly turned back to the wheel. As he did, he felt the right front tire drop from the pavement onto the gravel shoulder and heard gravel showering the truck. He gave the steering wheel a hard tug to the left in an attempt to get back on the road. For a split second, the truck didn't respond. Then the right front wheel met the jagged edge of the pavement and the tire exploded!

The next few seconds were a blur of violent reactions— headlights flashed rapidly to the left, then to the right, while a high-pitched screeching came from tires trying to grip the pavement.

Then the truck dipped and dived, seeming to float in slow motion as it rotated in the air.

Randy flew from the driver's side of the cab and crashed headlong into the passenger-side door. His jaw shattered, seven teeth were knocked out, and his neck broke. Then all the pain and feeling left as he lost consciousness.

Randy's unconscious body shot through the shattered passenger-side window as the truck flipped, catapulting him sixty feet into the air. When he landed, the impact broke his back in several places, shattering one vertebra.

Bone fragments showered his spinal cord. He lay deathly still.

The truck continued to roll and flip several times, finally coming to rest upside down in the middle of the road.

Almost immediately after the truck stopped rolling, Randy regained consciousness. His first reaction was to try to stand, but he couldn't move. Panic set in. He could see the truck not thirty feet away with its wheels still slowly turning. The inside lights were blinking on and off and the radio was blaring. Smoke clung to the ground like an eerie fog, and the smell of burning rubber filled his nostrils. Slowly, he realized that the truck's motor was still running. Then, with a cough, the motor died. Smoke belched up from around what appeared to be the hood—it was hard to tell for certain, since the truck was crushed beyond recognition. The lights blinked, dimmed, then went out.

Randy could hear his own heavy breathing in the quietness that surrounded him. His eyes clicked rapidly from side to side in an attempt to survey the wreck scene. Oddly, he became aware that he was lying in a patch of stickers. He could feel the prickle of the tiny burrs pressed against his cheek. It was then he began to realize what a perilous situation he was in.

Tears streamed across his blood-splattered face and intense emotion erupted.

"This is it, Lord—I've wrecked my new truck, I'm hurt so bad I can't move, and to top it all off, I've killed my dog!"

Randy's mind was whirling. He thought about his son. Brett was just nine years old and needed his father. He thought about his grandpa and parents, and about how the only time he ever prayed to God was when he wanted something.

"Dear God, I haven't lived the way you would have wanted me to. And I have made mistakes. But I have a family who depends on me. I need your guidance and help, dear Lord. I am going to die by myself on this lonely road if you don't help me. I guess I've cashed in my chips this time— and I have no one to blame but myself."

Randy slipped into silence. There was nothing left to be said.

He had sometimes wondered when and where the end would come. It had never entered his mind that it would be on a lonely stretch of road on a cold winter night. He had been injured while riding broncs, but had always walked away. This time was different—he couldn't walk away.

Then a clear voice pierced the silence.

"Randy, if you are going to live through this, you have to keep your eyes on me."

"What... who's there?" Randy called.

He attempted to move once more, but failed. He peered into the darkness, straining to locate the voice, but could see no one.

"Please help me," Randy pleaded.

As if from nowhere, Rooster licked him in the face.

"Where have you been? I thought you were dead!" Randy sobbed.

Rooster curled up next to his master.

A few minutes later, Randy felt that someone else was present. Out of the corner of his eye, he saw an old man standing about ten yards away. He stood completely still, looking down on Randy. He was dressed like an old cowboy, in a canvas-colored work coat that came down to his knees.

A large, wide-brimmed hat partially hid his gray-bearded face.

"Please sir, I need help," Randy pleaded.

The old man didn't respond.

"Please help me. I can't move."

The man stepped closer but still said nothing.

"Please, mister... I need help."

"I know you do, son. I have sent for help," the old man replied.

"Please call my grandpa," Randy asked.

But the man was gone.

Randy fell into despair.

Then, another man came and knelt next to him.

"How bad are you hurt?"

"I can't move, and my legs feel like balloons."

"I'll call an ambulance and get help," the man replied as he stood up.

"Please don't leave me," Randy pleaded.

"I won't leave you," the man said, as he turned and shouted to his wife to call the hospital and bring blankets. (The couple lived not far from the accident site and had heard the crash.)

"Please call my grandpa and tell him what has happened," Randy pleaded, giving him the telephone number.

"I will," the man replied, as he reached for Randy's hand.

"Where is the old man?" Randy asked.

"What old man?"

"There was an old man with a long coat and a wide-brimmed hat. He was here right before you arrived."

"I haven't seen anyone. And there hasn't been another car through here since we heard the accident."

"My God, what's happening to me? Am I dead? Is this a nightmare? Is any of this real?" Randy asked, before he lapsed into unconsciousness.

The woman returned from the house with an armload of blankets and the two quickly covered Randy.

"Is he alive?" the woman asked, as she held her trembling hands to her mouth.

"Yes, but he's hurt bad," the man replied, as he tucked the blankets tighter around Randy's broken body.

"Is the ambulance coming?"

"Yes. Oh Lord, I wish they'd hurry," the woman said in a trembling voice.

"He can't last much longer; he's busted up on the inside, and he told me he can't move," the man whispered.

They waited in silence.

The ambulance siren could be heard long before its flashing lights appeared. It was a mournful sound that disturbed the silence of the early morning. The man stepped into the road, frantically waving as he walked. The ambulance slowed to a stop as the man pointed to where Randy lay.

Randy regained consciousness and seemed alert as the paramedics grabbed their lifesaving equipment and rushed to his side.

With all of the lights flashing and people moving quickly about, Rooster was disturbed and leapt to his feet, growling in defense of his injured master.

"Hush, Rooster, it's all right," Randy whispered.

Rooster resumed his defensive position next to Randy.

The first paramedic to reach Randy knelt next to him. His trained eyes took inventory of Randy's condition: an obviously shattered jaw, possible internal bleeding. He pulled the blankets back far enough to see the strange position of Randy's neck and shoulders. He quickly covered him back up.

"What's your name?" the paramedic asked.

He needed to draw Randy into conversation, not only to get his name so the hospital could contact his relatives, but to further determine his condition.

"Randy Bird."

"Can you move?"

"No."

The other paramedic knelt beside Randy, pulled the blankets back, and began the process of checking Randy's vital signs.

"Please call my grandpa," Randy requested. (Randy's grandpa had always been his security.) "If he were here," Randy thought, "he would know what to do."

The second paramedic gave the other a concerned glance.

"Let's get him stabilized and transport him immediately. We can't help him here."

The paramedics immobilized Randy, then carefully moved him onto a backboard and strapped him down. They snapped a c-collar around his neck and his head and taped it to the backboard. They lifted him onto the stretcher and quickly carried him to the ambulance.

The couple watched, feeling completely helpless, as the paramedics tended to Randy. The woman shivered in the cold morning air, and her husband pulled her close while the paramedics slid Randy into the ambulance.

The siren of another emergency vehicle shattered the night and, within seconds, a Texas Highway Patrol car pulled to a stop. A trooper emerged, pulling his coat on as he walked to the ambulance.

"What have we got?" he asked, glancing in at Randy.

"Bad one," one of the paramedics replied, as he climbed into the ambulance.

"Get us to Greenville quick as you can!" the other paramedic said to the trooper.

"You got it," he replied, moving toward his car. He stopped, turned and shouted to the couple, "I'll need a statement. Where do you live?"

"In the brick house right over there," the man said, pointing. The trooper quickly jerked the keys from the ignition and ran to the rear of the car. He grabbed a handful of flares and placed them around the wreck. He turned the cruiser around in the middle of the road. With tires squealing and siren blasting, he pulled around the ambulance.

The couple stood for a moment watching the emergency vehicles disappear. In seconds they were out of sight and soon all was quiet. The couple slowly walked toward their house. They had done all they could. It was up to others now.

The ambulance driver contacted the hospital in Greenville and described Randy's condition as best he could. He knew the hospital staff would be ready for Randy by the time the ambulance arrived. Nonetheless, he felt tense. He had seen many accident victims in his years as a paramedic, but he would never get used to it.

The two emergency vehicles pulled off the winding farm-to-market road, up the service road, and onto Interstate 30. The driver was pushing the ambulance to its limits. Time was critical for Randy's survival.

In the back of the ambulance, the paramedic could do no

more than monitor Randy's vital signs and try to keep him awake with conversation. Randy's alertness would help the hospital staff evaluate his condition.

"Call my grandpa," Randy said, repeating the telephone number.

"The hospital will," the paramedic replied.

"He'll know what to do," Randy said, more to himself than the paramedic.

"Tell the hospital to call his grandpa," the paramedic shouted to the driver, calling out the telephone number Randy had given him.

Then Randy lost consciousness.

Chapter 3

The ambulance lights cast dancing shadows on the concrete walls of the hospital. The double-glass emergency room doors flew open and two white-clad nurses rushed through.

"How bad is it?" one asked.

"Bad," the paramedic replied, opening the ambulance's rear door.

Randy was carefully moved from the ambulance. As the procession started briskly down the hall, a doctor arrived and began assessing Randy's condition.

"What happened?" the doctor asked.

"Single-vehicle accident. Truck flipped over, throwing him out. It doesn't appear that the truck rolled over him, but we can't be sure," the paramedic answered.

The other paramedic listed Randy's vital signs.

"I want a lateral c-spine X-ray immediately," the ER doctor ordered.

The younger nurse began cutting Randy's boots off.

Randy was rushed to the Radiology Department where X-rays confirmed the staff's fears. There were multiple spinal fractures and the spinal cord was seriously damaged.

"Contact Methodist Hospital. Explain what we have and

get the physician on call to accept the patient. Then make arrangements for CareFlite to transport—and hurry!" the ER doctor told the senior nurse.

"Has anyone contacted his grandfather?" one of the paramedics asked.

"We haven't," the senior nurse replied. "Did the Highway Patrol trooper contact anyone?"

"No, he didn't know who to call."

"I'll call now," she said, pulling out a rumpled piece of paper the ambulance driver had given her earlier.

She dialed the number with a sinking feeling. This was the part of her job she always dreaded. Too many times she had had to wake up relatives in the middle of the night to tell them their loved ones were in serious condition. The phone rang once, twice. Then a man's voice answered.

The nurse asked, "Is this Mr. Barefield, Randy Bird's grandfather?"

"Yes."

"Mr. Barefield, this is Citizens General Hospital in Greenville. Randy has been seriously injured in a car accident."

"I'll be there in ten minutes."

"No, Mr. Barefield, don't come here. Randy will be moved to Methodist Hospital in Dallas by CareFlite helicopter. It would be best to go straight there."

"Thank you for calling."

Pa, as Randy called his grandfather, told his wife what had happened, and then called Randy's mother who lived in Oklahoma City. He glanced at the clock as he dressed. It was 4:30 a.m.

Randy lay immobile, waiting in the emergency room for

transportation to Methodist Hospital. Both paramedics moved back against the walls of the ER examination room. Their job was done.

"He won't make it," one whispered to the other.

His partner nodded in agreement.

Randy was accepted as a spinal-cord trauma patient by Methodist Hospital. With the CareFlite helicopter en route, all that was left to do now was wait.

A young ER doctor stood next to Randy's motionless form, watching the heart monitor. The graph marched relentlessly across the screen. The senior nurse stood on Randy's other side with her arms folded. Other than the steady beep, beep, beep of the heart monitor, the room was quiet.

Feeling a need for action, she removed the covers from Randy's right arm, slipped the blood pressure sleeve in place, and began pumping.

The examination room door flew open and a young nurse said urgently, "Doctor, accident victims incoming."

The doctor glanced at Randy, then at the senior nurse.

"Stay with him. Call if you need me."

He hurried out the door.

The nurse stood a few minutes longer, then pulled up a chair next to Randy. She studied his blood-splattered, youthful face. Her eyes filled and tears began to roll down her cheeks. "Be objective, be objective," she repeated to herself.

She had seen so many injuries. It seemed never to end. "Maybe it's time to leave emergency room duty, or maybe it's time to quit nursing altogether," she thought. Reaching for Randy's hand, she bowed her head. "I hope you are a

Christian, young man. You're going to need all the help you can get to whip this."

All was silent except for the beep, beep, beep.

"Helicopter coming," a voice shouted from the hall.

A procession of nurses quickly pushed Randy from the ER entrance to the helicopter landing pad as the giant helicopter came to rest. The rotor blades began to turn more slowly, then finally stopped. The door slid back and Randy was lifted into the open bay.

"Good luck," the senior nurse shouted. The motor whined and the giant rotor blades began to turn, slowly at first, then faster. Everything within yards of the helicopter that wasn't tied down seemed to be airborne. Paper and dead grass circled above the helicopter, then vanished. One almost expected to see cars in the parking lot begin to rotate. The flashing lights, flying particles, and the overpowering noise of the rotor blades made the helicopter departure an awesome event.

The first glow of approaching sunrise was barely visible as the helicopter lights disappeared over the horizon.

Two paramedics and a pilot were aboard the CareFlite helicopter as it hurtled towards Dallas and the Methodist Hospital. Randy was already being monitored by on-board instruments and his condition forwarded to the hospital. Estimated arrival time was twenty minutes. Time was critical.

"Fibrillating!" one of the paramedics shouted over the helicopter noise.

The other paramedic responded by preparing to give Randy's heart an electric shock. He held the paddles on opposite sides of Randy's bare chest.

"Clear!" he shouted.

Randy shook violently as the electric current pulsed through his body.

Again, then again. Then the welcome beep, beep, beep became audible. The paramedic took a deep breath and laid the paddles back in the black case as he glanced at the heart monitor graph.

Although unconscious, Randy sensed his surroundings: the reflection of lights, similar to multicolored strobe lighting, and the impression of three bunks stacked one on one in the bay of the helicopter. It was only a fleeting sense, while he seemed to be floating through air. Then darkness surrounded him once more.

On arrival at Methodist Hospital, Randy was rushed from the helicopter to the ER by a team of nurses and doctors who specialized in trauma treatment. Placed onto a Stryker frame, Randy was strapped between its two flat surfaces which could be rotated to allow examination from different angles without risk of causing further damage.

Pa arrived at the hospital only minutes after Randy was moved to the emergency room. He was told that the trauma team was trying to determine the extent of Randy's injuries and that a doctor would talk to him as soon as possible.

Meanwhile, Randy's mother, Betty Watson, had rushed to the airport in Oklahoma City to catch a flight to Love Field in Dallas. Her brother-in-law met her, and they arrived at Methodist Hospital at 6:30 a.m., only two hours after she had received Pa's call.

She saw her father sitting alone in the waiting room with his head bowed. He had always been their tower of strength and the one the family turned to in trying times. He would know what to do. She cried as he embraced her.

"Where's Randy?" she asked, tears coursing down her face.

"They're running tests and taking X-rays," Pa answered.

"Have you seen him?" she asked, glancing down the hall.

"No, all I know is what the nurse said when she called me from the hospital in Greenville."

Betty sat on the edge of the couch as Pa walked back and forth. After what seemed an eternity, a doctor appeared.

"Are you Mr. Bird's relatives?"

"Yes, I'm his mother, and this is his grandfather, Mr. Barefield," Betty said, gesturing to Pa.

"Mrs. Bird, your son is in very serious condition. He has suffered multiple fractures to his neck and spine, and there is damage to the spinal cord."

Betty and Pa heard what the doctor said, but it seemed distant and unreal. This couldn't be happening, not to Randy. He had played football, run track, and rodeoed. They'd always thought he was indestructible.

The doctor continued, "I realistically can't offer anything more positive than that we'll do everything we can to save your son's life."

"Save his life!" Betty answered, startled.

Pa put his arms around his daughter as she stared at the doctor in disbelief.

"I'm sorry. I'll keep you informed as soon as we know more," the doctor said softly, as he turned and walked back down the hall.

After the initial shock, Betty told Pa that they had to contact Randy's father and her other son, James Bird, and her daughter, Peggy.

Betty contacted Randy's father, Jim Bird, at his home in

Terrell, Texas, informing him of the accident and Randy's critical condition.

Peggy lived in Fort Worth, but she was out of town and they were unable to contact her.

As Jim drove the forty miles from Terrell to Methodist Hospital, he prayed for Randy's recovery and reflected on his youngest son's competitiveness and desire to excel in whatever he pursued. Randy had always been a fierce competitor in sports, even though he was usually the smallest player on the team. He had found out early in life that if you were small you had to play with more desire and determination. As a result, Randy would push himself harder than any coach could.

Jim Bird had a peaceful feeling as he approached the hospital. Somehow he knew Randy would survive. With God's healing hands and Randy's determination, he would recover.

Once he had arrived and parked the car, Jim rushed to the ER waiting room where Betty and Pa anxiously waited for the doctor's report.

Meanwhile, Betty had been calling James, Randy's brother. James was the oldest, and the two brothers had been close all their lives. He would take it hard, Betty thought, as she dialed the phone. James lived in Katy, Texas, and worked on an offshore oil platform in the gulf. He worked two weeks on the job, then had two weeks off. On his two weeks off he worked part time for a car dealership. He was at the dealership when the call came from his wife about the accident.

Betty called James' home at about 9:00 a.m. and told his wife, Becky, that Randy had been in an accident and wasn't expected to live. Becky immediately contacted James.

"Becky, what's wrong?" James asked.

"Randy has been in an accident," she sobbed.

"How bad is it?" James asked, his chest tightening.

"Bad… he's not expected to live."

James' pulse quickened and he could almost feel the blood race throughout his body. It was a cold morning and all of a sudden he was uncomfortably hot. His legs momentarily buckled. But he grabbed hold of a chair and straightened up. He knew he had to regain control if he was to be any help to his mother and Randy.

"What hospital is he at?" James asked.

"Dallas Methodist," Becky replied.

"Get me on an airplane—I'll be home in a minute."

James hung up the phone and ran to his car, not even taking the time to tell his employer he was leaving. As he drove home, vivid memories of his and Randy's childhood flooded his mind.

He remembered how hard it had been growing up as children of a minister. Their behavior had to be beyond reproach, and for young, energetic boys, that wasn't always an easy task. After reaching adulthood, they had both attempted to experience the things they felt had been denied them as children. That, in combination with the divorce of their parents, had affected them. They had both strayed from their religious upbringing.

James remembered the days they had spent riding horses and making big plans to be rodeo stars as only the young can do. Now it seemed that all he would have were those memories… his brother was dying… his friend and constant childhood companion would not be there anymore… and it was more than he could stand. He sobbed uncontrollably.

Back at the hospital, the others waited anxiously. It was mid-morning before the doctor returned, accompanied by a specialist who confirmed the original diagnosis. Randy was at extreme risk.

"Can we see him?" Betty asked.

"Yes, but I am not sure you should," the doctor replied.

"He's unconscious," the specialist said. "But it's up to you."

Betty and Pa followed the doctors to the examination room. Both thought their hearts would beat out of their chests. This was something that happened to other people, not to them. They had always lived Christian lives. Randy's father and grandfather were both ministers. It just couldn't be happening to them.

They entered the room.

Randy was suspended face-down, secured between the firm support of the Stryker boards. Blood dripped slowly from his shattered jaw. They couldn't see anything of his face other than a bloody profile.

Fear such as she had never known gripped Betty. Her hands went to her mouth in an attempt to stifle the scream that welled up from deep inside. Her eyes filled with tears as she turned to Pa for support.

Pa looked at the still form of his grandson and shuddered. Randy had always been the active one. He loved everything about life. It was hard to imagine him so still, so quiet.

The specialist broke the silence.

"Mrs. Bird, your son will not survive seventy-two hours. I am sorry to be so blunt, but I don't know what else to say."

Betty turned away from Pa and faced the doctor.

"If that's the way you feel, then we'll move Randy to

another hospital and find another doctor."

"Mrs. Bird, if you attempt to move him, he will die for certain," the doctor replied as he walked toward the door.

Randy had slowly become aware of voices. His eyes would not focus and all he could make out was a blur of light. Then he heard his mother's voice and he felt a twinge of excitement. He heard the doctor tell his mother that he wouldn't live through the night and something inside him gave him the strength to speak.

"I'm not dead yet," Randy whispered in a rasping but audible voice.

The doctor jerked his head around in surprise.

Betty bent over to where she could see Randy's face, wiping the tears from her eyes.

"How do you feel?"

"I can't feel nothing, Mama. But I'm not dead, and I'm not going to die. Where's Pa?

"Right here, son."

"Help me, Pa," Randy sobbed.

"I will, Randy, and so will the Lord. No matter what anyone says, you are going to live," Pa replied, with tears running down his face.

James arrived around noon and went directly to the ICU waiting room. When he saw his parents and grandfather, emotion engulfed him.

"Mama, I'm so sorry," James cried as he embraced his mother.

Pa stood and put his arms around his grandson and daughter.

"Randy's going to be all right," Pa said softly. "He's a

fighter and the Lord has other plans for him."

James was relieved. Pa was the rock, the catalyst that held the family together. If Pa, a former Baptist minister, said Randy was going to be all right, then he would.

Hours became days. Days seemed like years, and the nights like eternity. The first twenty-four hours passed, then forty-eight, with no change in Randy's condition. From time to time, he would regain consciousness only to drift away. Betty and Pa left the hospital for only a few hours at a time to bathe and rest.

James reluctantly returned to the gulf for his two-week shift, returning immediately afterward. It became a routine that continued for almost two years.

At one point, Randy regained consciousness long enough to call for his mother.

"Mama, are you there?"

"Yes, Randy, I'm here," she replied, moving closer.

"Pray for me, Mama," he sobbed.

"I am, Randy. God is with you, remember that."

"Mama, I'm so sick. Where is Pa?"

"He's just outside. I'll get him."

Randy didn't answer. He had drifted away.

Betty returned to her chair.

Seventy-two hours came and went, and Randy Bird was still alive.

Chapter 4

Nine long days had passed since the first critical seventy-two hours, and Randy's condition remained the same. Betty maintained a night-and-day vigil, a practice she would continue for three months. She and Pa watched helplessly as Randy seemed to slowly slip away from them. Throughout, Pa maintained his constant optimism, however, encouraging Randy at every opportunity. But inside, even he was beginning to feel worn down.

Finally, on the tenth day, after surgery had been canceled and rescheduled four times, Betty and Pa were told that Randy's surgery would be later that day. The procedure was complicated and would take a long time, the doctor said.

Once more, Betty and Pa were not given any hope that Randy would survive. If by some miracle he did survive the surgery, they were told, he would be completely paralyzed.

Betty and Pa would not accept such a negative diagnosis. They had to be positive, not only for themselves and the rest of the family, but for Randy.

The surgery went as well as could be expected. All they could do now was wait. Only time would tell what condition Randy would be in.

Several hours after the surgery, Betty knelt beside Randy,

desperate to hear her son speak.

"Randy, can you hear me?"

Randy's face twitched, but his eyes remained closed.

"Can you hear me?" she repeated.

"Yes, ma'am, I hear you," Randy whispered, opening his eyes.

"How do you feel?"

"I can't feel anything, except my back is burning like fire. Am I all right?"

"You're fine," Betty replied, as she straightened up and wiped the tears from her swollen eyes. "You rest now."

Randy closed his eyes.

In the first days after the surgery, Randy was completely immobilized with straps and mechanical restraints. After swelling from the surgery subsided, he was put in a body cast from his neck to his upper thighs to further restrict any movement.

Randy could speak when he wasn't vomiting, but the tubes that went up through his nostrils and into his stomach were a constant irritation. The antiseptic smell mixed with odors from his own body secretions seemed to overwhelm Randy, adding to his nausea. He pleaded for the nurses to check the catheter and diaper, but he was just one of several patients in ICU and his concerns went unattended. He voiced his concerns to his mother when she was allowed to visit him in ICU.

"Mama, I smell so bad. I believe my stomach would get better if it didn't smell so bad in here."

Betty pulled the sheet back, careful not to disturb the catheter. Her hands shook as she unfastened the diaper. She gasped when she saw that Randy was lying in his own feces and that it had dried to his skin. Disbelief turned to anger as she approached the head nurse at the nurses' station outside ICU.

"Did you know that Randy is lying in his own feces and it is stuck to him? He had to have been like that for hours!" Betty shouted.

"We can't be right there every time something happens. We have more patients than Randy," the head nurse replied.

"I don't care how many patients you have. For the amount this hospital is charging, there should be three nurses for Randy. I want him taken care of or I'll do it myself," Betty said, folding her arms and staring at the head nurse.

"You can't do that. It's against hospital regulations."

"I don't care about hospital regulations. I want Randy taken care of, and I want it done right now."

"I'll get someone to clean him up right away."

"I am staying with him from now on whether you or the hospital likes it or not," Betty said, as she hurried back to Randy's bedside, leaving the head nurse standing.

In a few minutes, a young nurse came. She immediately began cleaning Randy. Then came the head nurse and the hospital administrator.

"These things happen occasionally. It is due to understaffing rather than neglect. It won't happen again," the administrator said.

"It sure won't happen again, because I am going to stay right here. I know it's just a job to most of the people that work here, but this is my son, and I am going to see to him," Betty responded firmly.

"We have explained that that is not possible."

"I am staying," a determined Betty replied.

The nurses and administrator left without another word.

Later, Betty learned that the staff members were told not to interfere with her and to let her stay with Randy as long as she wanted. Betty never left Randy's bedside the entire time he was at Methodist Hospital.

Unbeknownst to Randy, news of his accident and critical condition was spreading throughout the Christian community. Many churches in the northern part of Texas— from Greenville to Tomball—were praying for Randy. People he had never met, as well as his many friends, came to the hospital by the dozens just to let Randy and his family know they cared. Many would sleep on the floor in the waiting room. They knew they couldn't see him in ICU, but hoped their presence and prayers would give Randy and his family strength.

His rodeo cowboy friends filed in one or two at a time. They would stand politely against the waiting room wall. Holding their wide-brimmed hats in their hands, they would bow their heads, then leave as quietly as they had come.

If a man's worth could be judged by the friends he had, Randy Bird was a rich man indeed.

Randy's father visited him several times a week, offering prayers and encouragement. It hurt Jim more than anyone knew to see his son lying there, knowing there wasn't anything he could do except pray for him.

Peggy Sue, Randy's sister, also visited whenever she was in town.

Randy's days and nights were spent staring at the ceiling or the floor, according to how he was positioned. He began to identify his visitors by the shoes or boots they wore.

He felt helpless. He had completely lost control of his life. He no longer had control over his body and all the decisions about his life were being made by someone other than himself. He didn't even know who was taking care of his horses and dogs—if anyone was. He wondered how Brett was doing and what he thought was happening to his father.

Brett had been only four when Randy and Brett's mother had separated and divorced. Randy said it was because both of them were immature and too stubborn to compromise. But none of their problems had affected their love for Brett.

Somehow he had to let his son know that everything would be all right, so Randy asked Betty to bring Brett to see him.

The next day, Brett walked close beside his grandmother as they approached Randy in ICU.

"Randy, Brett's here," Betty said.

Randy opened his eyes to see Brett.

"Come here, son. I can't see you over there."

Brett cautiously moved closer.

"It's all right, son. Your daddy is going to be fine. I want you to know that."

"I know," he replied quietly.

"I'll be out of here before you know it."

"Yes, sir," Brett answered, looking around at all the equipment and tubes everywhere. Randy's condition and the whole setup of the ICU overwhelmed him. For a ten-year-old boy, seeing is believing. His father didn't look or sound like himself. Randy's jaw and face were still swollen, and further surgery was scheduled for three days later.

"Can I take a walk with Grandmother?" Brett asked.

"Sure, they won't let you stay long anyhow. I love you."

"I love you too, Daddy."

Brett didn't say a word until they were outside the hospital.

"Is my daddy going to die?" he asked, looking at his grandmother.

"No, he is not," Betty replied.

"How will we get money to live on?"

It startled Betty to hear Brett ask such an adult question.

"Don't you worry about that; it's all been taken care of."

After Brett left, Randy sobbed uncontrollably until there were no more tears. He felt as if God had deserted him. He had never felt so alone in his life. Maybe the doctors were right—maybe there was no hope.

Then Pa came in and sat beside him.

"Pa, I'm going to die," Randy sobbed.

"No, you're not," Pa replied in a stern voice.

"Pa, you're going to think I'm crazy, but I've got something to tell you."

"Then tell me."

"When I was lying in the ditch after the accident, God spoke to me. He told me to look to him and I would live. And Pa, there was an angel came to my side. He was dressed like an ol' cowboy, but he was an angel for sure."

"I don't think you're crazy, son," Pa replied, his voice breaking.

"Pa, I have been a bargaining Christian all my life, and that's why God has given up on me."

"What do you mean by that?"

"Every time I needed the Lord's help, I would make deals with him. But as soon as I got what I wanted, or the crisis was over, I would go right back to living just like before."

"Remember what God said when you lay in that ditch?"

"Yes, sir."

"He is with you now. And you are not going to die. Don't ever think that again. God loves you," Pa said, as he held Randy's hand.

Randy drifted off to sleep.

A few days had passed. Randy lay in his hospital bed, straining with all his might to move. He thought if he could just force one movement—anything at all—he could prove that all the doctors were wrong.

It was during one of the times he was straining to move that he felt a slight tingling sensation in his right index finger.

"Mama, I can move my finger!" he shouted. Betty leapt to her feet and stood next to Randy.

"Let me see!"

Randy strained, but the finger didn't move. He strained harder. Then out of the corner of his eye, he saw the finger twitch, then slowly curl.

"Oh my God! It did move!" Betty shouted.

"Tell Pa."

Betty raced from the room to locate Pa and tell him the news.

Randy looked at the blank white ceiling through

tear-filled eyes.

"Thank you, Lord," he whispered.

Soon he was able to move his left index finger, then touch his thumb with his index finger, and then, he could move his head more freely. It didn't seem like much to anyone else, but to Randy, it was a step toward recovery.

He soon got to the point of being able to take round, colored pegs of a rehabilitation "toy" and place them in holes of a matching color. He would do this all day. He was getting better.

Pa was Randy's cheerleader. Every time Randy moved or tried something, anything, Pa was there to cheer him on. One time Randy saw his foot move.

"Pa, my foot moved," he shouted.

"It sure did," Pa agreed, even though he had been looking away at the time.

Where Pa was the problem solver and motivator, Nanny, Randy's maternal grandmother, was the healer and peacemaker. She was a frequent visitor to the hospital and, when she realized that it would take more than love and caring to make him well, she was devastated. She would sit and hold Randy's hand for hours, sobbing. Finally, Randy told Pa that it was just too hard on her and that it would be better if she didn't come for a while, at least until he was improving.

Randy would lie for hours looking at the ceiling and thinking about everything. Mostly he thought about the past; the future was still too uncertain to consider.

One time, he thought about when Pa had arranged a

family reunion at the Trinity Valley Ranch. After everyone had eaten and visited, Pa had told the grandchildren to get their fathers and come with him. There were saddled horses waiting for them, and they all rode to where several cowboys were holding a herd of horses in a small valley. Pa told the children to pick a horse, any horse. It would be theirs to keep.

Randy and his brother, James Ray, looked at each other and immediately began whispering. They decided to ask Pa to let them look the horses over and each get a mare with a foal. That way, they could each get two horses.

Pa gave them permission to ride into the herd. He told them that, since James was the oldest grandchild and Randy the second oldest, they would get the first and second choices.

James picked a gray mare that had a palomino colt, and Randy picked out an appaloosa mare with a colt at her side. To a twelve-year-old boy, this was the greatest day of his life.

Randy owned many horses after that, but no two were ever as special as the mare and colt that Pa had given him.

Randy's jaw and face surgery was scheduled for eight o'clock in the evening, two weeks after the back surgery. It was supposed to last an hour. In due time, he was wheeled off to surgery, and the family waited anxiously. By midnight, no one had told them anything. They knew only that he was still in surgery.

At six o'clock the next morning, the surgeon approached the family.

"Randy had a blood clot. The clot caused a mild stroke," the surgeon said quietly.

"Is he OK?" Betty asked, tears running down her face.

"We don't know if there is further damage or not. We'll just have to wait and see."

"I want to see him," Betty said.

"He's in Recovery. You can see him later. You all look like you could use some rest."

By mid-morning, Betty demanded to see Randy and was led to his bedside. Randy couldn't move anything but his eyes. His jaw was wired shut and his face swollen beyond recognition. Betty looked down at her youngest son and wondered how much more he could take. The nurse told Betty she would have to leave, but Randy's pleading eyes asked her to stay.

"I am not going anywhere," Betty replied.

"It's not up to me," the nurse replied.

"I don't care who it's up to. This is my son and he needs me. I am not leaving him now or any other time until he leaves this hospital."

After several discussions between hospital staff and administrators, it was decided Betty could remain. And remain she did, for another three months.

Randy could move only his eyes. The stroke had left him completely paralyzed. He no longer had control over any of his bodily functions. What movement he had had before the operation was gone. His worst nightmare had become a reality.

Chapter 5

The family was told that Randy would be completely paralyzed for the rest of his life, and the quicker they all accepted that, the sooner they would be in a position to help Randy accept it.

Randy could only stare at the ceiling and think. His eyes were all he could move. He thought about anything that would make the time pass faster. He remembered every horse he had ever owned and every rodeo he had ever ridden in. He imagined himself riding bareback broncs and going to the national cutting finals. He thought about what Brett and he were going to do with the ranch. In his imagination, they even built a big show barn and roping pen.

He remembered how he came to own Watch Joe. He had leased two of his mares to a friend, Roger Glover. One of the mares had a good-looking, muscled-up sorrel colt. The first time Randy saw the colt, he knew the little sorrel was going to be special. Even at the age of three months, the colt would snort and run off with his tail in the air when someone tried to approach him.

One day when Randy was showing the horses to Pa, they drove past the field where the two mares and their foals were pastured. Randy noticed that the sorrel colt was standing motionless next to his mother. His head was dropped down and one hind leg was pulled up under him.

"Something's wrong with that colt," Randy remarked, as he stopped the truck.

He and Pa approached the colt slowly so as to not spook him. The colt didn't attempt to run, which was unusual.

"My God... look at that hole in his chest!" Randy exclaimed, pointing at a gaping hole in the right front part of the colt's chest.

Closer investigation revealed another hole in his stomach. Parts of his tiny intestines were hanging out.

"He's been shot by a high-powered rifle," Randy said.

"Sure looks like it," Pa agreed.

They hurried back to the ranch, hooked on the trailer, and drove back. They managed to load the mare so the colt would follow. They drove to the veterinary clinic at Rockwall and called Roger Glover to meet them there.

After examination, the veterinarian told Randy the most humane thing to do would be to put the colt down. He would never be any good, even if he lived.

Randy told the vet to wait until Roger got there, since it was his colt.

When Roger saw the extent of the injury, he agreed with the vet.

"If you're going to put him down, let me have him," Randy said.

"I've got six hundred dollars in stud fees and mare care for a year in that colt," Roger replied.

"Hey, you've got nothing if you put him down," Randy rationalized. "And I'll foot the bill for his treatment."

Roger thought a minute.

"OK, I guess you're right."

Randy left the colt at the clinic for about ten days, then he picked up the baby horse. He was still in bad shape: his legs looked like gigantic balloons with hooves attached. Once home, Randy removed the partition between two stalls in the horse barn and turned the colt in there.

Every morning, he would get up early and clean the colt's wounds with water, then run a solution that Pa had given him completely through the hole. This went on for several months. Finally, the colt healed completely. The only sign left of the major wound was a scar the size of a quarter. But the colt would still hop on his front feet rather than move them individually, and he would never lie down.

When the colt was almost a year old, Randy decided it was time to find out once and for all if the sorrel was ever going to be normal. He haltered the colt and walked him to the round pen beside the barn. Randy stood there holding the lead rope for several minutes. He dreaded what he had to do. This colt thought Randy was his mother. He trusted Randy, and Randy was going to have to whip him.

Randy sighed as he slipped the halter off the colt, which he had named Watch Joe. The colt moved away with his hopping gait. Randy popped the whip and Watch Joe quickened his speed, but was still hopping.

Randy moved closer and swung the whip, snapping it across the sorrel's bottom. The colt's stride quickened and his eyes grew wide. He couldn't understand why the man who had nursed and fed him every day for a year was whipping him.

Randy bit his lip and swung the whip harder than before. Watch Joe leapt forward. He reached out with his front feet and broke into a full run. After that, he never hopped again.

Randy broke in the sorrel at eighteen months. When Watch Joe was close to three, Randy took him to the veterinarian who had treated him after the injury.

Watch Joe had a better than average handle on him. So when Randy unloaded him at the clinic, he jumped up on him bareback, with no gear but the halter on. When the vet came out, Randy spun Watch Joe around, jumped him off a few feet and skidded him to a sliding stop. Randy stepped off and walked up to the vet.

"What do you think about that little gelding?" Randy asked, smiling.

"I'd say he was a pretty good handling kind of a horse."

"Do you remember this horse?" Randy asked.

"No, I sure don't."

"You treated him some time back."

"I sure don't remember him."

"Remember the colt that had been shot?"

"Naw, that can't be him."

"Sure is."

"Well, he's sure come a long way."

Watch Joe was an exceptional horse. "Maybe, just maybe," Randy thought as he lay paralyzed, "I'll be able to ride him again someday."

Finally, Randy began to be able to move again. First a finger, then a hand, then his head.

But infections started, and the sickness intensified.

Randy would count off the minutes and hours, hoping

that the end of another day would bring him closer to regaining his health.

With his jaw still wired shut, he had a hard time making people understand him, but when anyone came within hearing distance, he asked them the time. Every minute that passed meant a minute closer to feeling good again. At night he would pray for God to give him the strength to make it to the next day.

His weight was down to one hundred pounds. He had weighed 160 at the time of the accident, and had been bench-pressing three hundred pounds.

He got to the point where he wanted to be better so badly that he began to lie to everyone, telling them he was feeling better than he really was. If willing himself healthy could cure a person, Randy Bird would be well.

He was totally dependent on others and he was told repeatedly that he would always have to rely on others for help.

For a person who had been independent for more than ten years, the thought of such dependence was devastating. Randy would stare at the ceiling and cry for hours at a time. But then he would think about other scenarios. What if it had been Brett, or his parents, or Pa, or Pa's wife, Nanny, who had been hurt? It was then he stopped asking why it had happened to him, and became thankful that it was he who had been hurt and not his loved ones.

Randy also began to be more positive about his recovery and pushed himself even harder. He would look at his toes and strain until the blood vessels in his neck stood out, but nothing happened. There was no movement at all.

What made it all worse was that it seemed to Randy that

whatever positive things he did were met with pessimism from the staff. Pa was his only ray of hope.

Betty, after endless days and nights, had reached the point of exhaustion. As a loving parent, she had been living through her worst nightmare. There was nothing she could do for Randy except be there. So she sat for hours, wondering what Randy would do after he left the hospital. It was obvious he would never regain the use of his legs. He would need constant care and special facilities. Her spirits sank. She could never remember being so tired.

One day when Randy's optimism was low, he turned to his mother.

"Mama, why can't you be here for me?" he asked quietly, as tears filled his eyes.

"Randy, I am here for you," Betty replied, moving next to his bed.

"I don't mean that, Mama. But surely, if you believed I was going to get well and you were praying for me, I would get well."

"Son, I pray for you every day of my life," she said, as tears rolled down her cheeks. "You will get well. I am sure of it."

She held Randy's hand until he closed his eyes and drifted off.

The infections intensified and Randy was sick constantly. The body cast only added to his discomfort. It was then he seemed to lose all hope.

Even though Pa still encouraged him and talked about the things they would do after Randy got out of the hospital, the constant sickness wore Randy to the point of exhaustion.

He fell into despair.

Then one day he saw a little boy, no more than four years old, who had sustained a head injury. The little boy was in a coma and his chances for recovery were not good.

Randy thought about the little boy for a long time. He thought of all the things the child would never experience. He would never know what it was like to go to school, to play baseball, or to fall in love, get married, and have a little boy of his own. Randy cried for that little boy and something wonderful began to happen to Randy. Unselfishly, he began to wish he could take the child's place.

This was a big step for Randy, who had always thought of himself as being bulletproof. He had played football in school and rodeoed most of his adult life. He had walked away from bronc-ride wrecks and even several car accidents— he had seemed invincible.

He had also seen himself as a caring, compassionate person. But when he saw the injured child, he began to realize he had felt compassion only when he was at a safe distance.

There was an awakening in Randy that day—an awareness and compassion for others that would continue to grow day by day. It became clear what he would do with the rest of his life—he would help people any way he could—he would make a difference.

From that moment on, Randy was determined to overcome whatever was thrown at him.

Some time later, the hospital staff moved Randy from ICU to a private room. As he lay there, Randy looked at the early May sun streaming though the hospital window, spilling its warm light across the tile floor. He stared into the brightness until he felt himself sinking down into despair. Trying to break the mood, Randy said, "Pa, talk to me. How are the horses and dogs doing?"

"They're all fine," Pa replied, sensing Randy's depression.

"Is the grass getting green?"

"Sure is."

"How are Ten and Watch Joe doing?"

"I think those two and Rooster miss you more than all the rest of the animals."

Randy turned his head to face Pa.

"Pa, I miss them so," he sobbed.

"I know you do, son. You'll be with them soon, you'll see."

"I'm not progressing. I'm standing still," Randy said, then smiled as he realized what he'd said. "Just a figure of speech," he added.

Pa smiled back.

"Did I ever tell you about what happened to Rooster right after the accident?"

"No, sir."

"About three days after the accident, someone called Nanny and told her that your dog was still at the accident scene and would not leave. No one could get him to come with them. So I drove down there, and sure enough, he was lying right where they picked you up that night. He was skin and bones, and his eyes were bloodshot. But he growled at me when I came close. I finally got him into the car by offering him food. He's doing fine now."

"He's something else," Randy said, remembering the little cowdog's snippy ways.

"But I believe ol' Watch Joe misses you more than any of them. He doesn't have the spunk he used to have. But when you get home, he'll brighten up," Pa added.

"Pa, I've got to move on. I can't just lie here. I'm not getting any better."

"They're talking about sending you to a place where you can start rehabilitation."

"When?"

"Well, I believe in a couple of weeks."

"I want to go now."

"Ask your mother about it after a while. She's been talking to the doctors about it."

"Pa, the doctors don't believe I'll get better."

"Randy, you just block all that out. They don't know you. You remember what God said to you, and keep looking to him. All things are possible through Jesus Christ."

"I know Pa, just keep reminding me."

They talked for hours until Betty came in and sat down.

"Mama, Pa said I was going to be moved to a place where they were going to help me get better."

"Yes, that's right," Betty replied. "I think it'll be Baylor. Their rehabilitation center is here in Dallas, and it's supposed to be one of the best."

Randy's spirit soared. He was going to make it. He was going to walk yet!

Chapter 6

The day finally arrived when Randy was to be moved to Baylor Rehabilitation Center. This would be the first real step toward recovery, and he was excited. The sooner he began physical therapy, the sooner he would be able to walk again.

The ride from Methodist Hospital to Baylor by ambulance was short, but it seemed endless to Randy. The steady movement and rolling motion of the ambulance made him sick at his stomach. After lying in a hospital room for three months staring at the floor or ceiling, the brightness of the sun was blinding, and it was frightening being out of the hospital confines. Even with a nurse accompanying him, he felt threatened and alone, much as he imagined a convict feels when released from prison.

After arriving at Baylor, Randy was taken directly to the elevator. When its door opened at the second floor, he was devastated. The hospital smell and atmosphere overwhelmed him. He glanced at the stark white floors and walls. This wasn't what he had expected. It was just another hospital!

He was taken to a semi-private room, where he vaguely remembers seeing someone lying in one of the beds. "This has to be a mistake," he thought. The place he was going to was supposed to be more like an athletic club, a place where he could regain the muscles he had lost and begin to walk again. It wasn't meant to be just another hospital, where they would poke pills down him and stick more tubes up his nose!

Randy lay on his back staring at the ceiling, while tears ran down his cheeks. He was emotionally drained.

"Lord, help me. I don't know what to do," Randy sobbed.

"Settled in yet?" James asked, as he and Pa came into the room.

"It's just another hospital," Randy replied, turning his head so he could see them. This was not an easy task, since a body cast still confined him from just above his thighs to his Adam's apple.

"It's not exactly another hospital, Randy. You still have to have medical care, but they're going to help you in other ways as well," Pa said, pulling a chair up next to Randy's bed.

"I don't need medical care, Pa. I just need to build up my strength so I can walk. I'll never get well lying in a bed. I just don't understand what's happening to me. Doesn't anyone give a damn?" Randy sobbed.

"Yes, they do. But it's a slow process. Just keep your faith and think positive. You are going to recover," Pa said, patting Randy on the arm.

"Yeah, you'll be up and around before you know it," James added.

"I want to know when. The doctors and nurses tell me I'll never walk again and everybody else says I will. I just want someone to tell me when!" Randy shouted, angry and frustrated. "Then I'm told I'm going to a place that's going to help me recover, and it looks and smells like the place I just left. Dammit, dammit, dammit," he sobbed.

"Randy, no one but God knows when you're going to walk again. The doctors and nurses don't know how strong you are on the inside, and God willing, you will walk again when you're ready," Pa said.

"I know, Pa. I know. I'm just so tired of not making any progress... It seems I'm going backward."

"That's not true," James said, moving closer to the bed. "If you remember, little brother, they didn't think you would live through the night. Well, here it is almost three months later and you're a long way from dead. You're not walking yet, but I'm willing to bet you soon will," he added, smiling.

"Yeah?... I suppose you're right," Randy replied. "And that reminds me... y'all have got to lighten up some on staying here. Pa, you and Mama have spent every day and night with me for three months and y'all have got to get away from here and get some rest. And James Ray, you've got a family to take care of. You can't keep coming up here all the time."

"Look, little brother, I have to work offshore two weeks out of the month, but there isn't anything going to keep me from being here those other two weeks. I might have to move Becky and the kids up here, but don't you worry about it. You've always been there for me and I can't do any less."

"Look y'all... somehow I've got to get control over my life. Someone other than myself is making all the decisions. I know all of you care and want the best for me. But when it comes down to it, I'm the one who has to make it work. From now on I want the doctors to talk to me. I'm an adult and capable of making my own decisions."

The next six weeks passed slowly and painfully. The body cast was a constant irritation to Randy and he voiced his discontent to everyone within hearing distance. For the first time in his life, Randy became pessimistic and uncontrollable. He shouted at the nurses, refused to take medicine, and generally made things as difficult as possible for all concerned.

It was easy for him to become depressed and angry. The people telling him what to do and how to do it were standing and walking. What did they know about being paralyzed? They didn't have any right to tell him anything! They could all walk into his room smiling and making small talk, then leave and go back to the outside world... the world Randy hadn't seen or been a part of for over four months. He stayed angry with everyone he came into contact with, except for Nancy.

Nancy was a short, heavy-set nurse with a smooth olive complexion, a soothing, soft Southern drawl, and a broad smile. Nancy became his confidante. He could ask her about things he couldn't talk about with other hospital staff members. Things were happening to him that he didn't understand, both mentally and physically, and Nancy was always there to help. She really seemed to care about Randy. She was the only hospital staff member who attempted to encourage him, even during the times when he was angry with everyone, including Nancy. She would tell him, "You're just hurting, honey. It'll get better." Randy found himself anticipating when Nancy's shift would begin.

One day when Randy was weak from constant infections and continual nausea, he spoke to his mother about his feelings.

"Mama."

"Yes, Randy, I'm here," Betty replied.

"Mama, what's going to happen to me?"

"You're going to get better. You've got to believe that or you'll never get well," Betty said, standing next to Randy.

"Mama, I'm thankful it's me instead of Brett or one of you," he sobbed.

"I know you are, son."

"Somehow we'll come through this, won't we?"

"Yes, we will... somehow."

"I used to think I could do anything. Is that the reason it happened to me?"

"No, terrible things happen to many people. Somehow they overcome them with faith and determination."

"I'll make it. I have to. There're people that depend on me."

Betty stood holding Randy's hand until he relaxed and drifted off to sleep.

Finally the day came when the body cast was to come off. Randy was excited at the prospect of its removal. Maybe things would get better now and he could begin his rehabilitation in earnest. Pa and Betty came earlier than usual and were sitting in Randy's room waiting with him.

"What's the weather like?" Randy asked.

"Typical June day—nice, cool mornings, turning warm by afternoon," Pa answered.

Randy stared out the window at the blue sky. He thought about the ranch and how everything must look and smell. The grass should be really green now and the horses all shedded and silky-looking. God, he wanted to be there.

More than anything, he wanted to be home...

"Mama, do you think I'll ever get well?" Randy asked.

He desperately needed reassurance.

"Of course you will," Betty said, as she reached for Randy's hand. "It will just take time."

"I'm tired of it taking time. I just want out of here. I want to go home, go back to work, and be able to ride my horses. That's not asking too much, is it?"

"No, son, that's not asking too much... and it'll happen. It's just going to take time. God is still in control," Pa replied.

After the cast was removed, Randy felt naked and totally without support. But he found he was able to move his arms and shoulders more, and that in itself was a positive step. With the cast off, he began limited physical therapy, and for the first time it seemed as if he were making real progress.

With nothing more to do than think most of the time, Randy became obsessed with the potential risk of fire. He expressed his concern to James about being on the second floor if fire broke out. He couldn't walk down the stairs and the elevators would not operate under emergency conditions. James would attempt to console Randy by reassuring him that he or Pa would be there to carry him out if necessary. But for several days it was on Randy's mind constantly.

One night, he began to shake uncontrollably after again telling James how concerned he was about not being able to escape a fire. James removed his shoes, pulled back the covers and lay next to his brother.

"Remember the time I broke my arm over at the Huckabees'? Mrs. Huckabee put me to bed until Mother and Daddy could get there. You got in bed with me, and when

Mother and Daddy got there, they couldn't tell which one had the broken arm because we both looked so terrible," James whispered, in an attempt to divert Randy's attention away from fires.

"Yeah, I remember," Randy replied, relaxing. "We were swinging out over a big stack of tires and dropping down into them. You missed and broke your arm. We couldn't have been over nine or ten."

"Yeah, it was a long time ago," James said.

"Remember when you broke your leg when that horse fell with you?" Randy asked.

"Yeah... I thought I was dead for sure that time. We've survived lots of wrecks, and somehow we'll survive this one," James said.

Randy and James spent many hours remembering things that had happened in their childhood. It kept Randy from having to think about the future.

Randy developed pressure sores and other complications due to loss of muscle and tissue. And he wasn't responding to treatment. So, after the surgeon explained the procedure, Randy was scheduled for more surgery, which would replace with healthy tissue the diseased skin caused by pressure sores.

The surgery was to be done at Baylor Medical. Randy would spend a short time in ICU, then be returned to his room at the rehabilitation center. Randy requested that Nancy accompany him. He felt that if Nancy were with him, he would have at least one person looking out for him.

Randy viewed the surgery as just one more setback in a series of them. He had come to the point of giving up and told Pa so.

"Randy, it's not in you to give up," Pa said.

"It doesn't make any difference what I do, something else happens to push me back down. I'm just tired of fighting."

"You're just worn down. You'll whip this. Give yourself time," Pa said.

Recovery from the surgery was slow and painful. Randy spent most of the time on his stomach. About the only therapy he received during this period was having his legs stretched and his still joints moved by the therapist.

A week after surgery, Randy was introduced to a four-wheeled gurney. On this, he could lie on his stomach and, with some tugging on the two front wheels, slowly move himself about. However, he didn't have the strength to propel himself far and he tired easily. But it was a positive step toward mobility.

Randy had several roommates at Baylor, some of whom stayed only a few days while others stayed for weeks. An Indian named Geronimo was one of those who stayed for weeks. Geronimo's reason for being there was that he had had hiccups for seven years. He couldn't speak English, so all instructions and conversations from the hospital staff had to be translated by a relative. Geronimo would drink gallons of water believing that this would help him, even though the doctors repeatedly told him not to. But he would drink and drink water until he would have a tremendous hiccup. Then out would fly all the water he had drunk... all over the walls, the bed, and on occasions, even Randy. After being sick at his stomach for three months, Randy found it more than he could stand. Geronimo would throw up all over the place and then Randy would follow. It wasn't a pretty sight.

Randy thought if he could just get out of the hospital and go home, he would heal. He pleaded with his family to take him home and finally the doctor agreed to let him go home for one day.

The following Sunday, Gary Mitchell and Press Parrish, two cowboy friends, borrowed a van and picked Randy up at the hospital. Randy had to lie face down on the gurney, but it did enable him to move about, and he could raise his head high enough to see out the window.

By the time they arrived at his grandparents' home, however, Randy was feeling weak and his stomach unsettled. Nanny fixed his favorite dish of fresh field peas, mashed potatoes, and iced tea.

All of Randy's family was there and Brett's mother, Donna, had brought Brett. It was like a homecoming for Randy. He managed to eat a small amount of food and kept telling Nanny how good everything was throughout dinner.

After dinner Randy wanted to go see his ranch. He hadn't seen the place since the day before the accident. His friends agreed to drive him there and got him situated in the van.

As the van came slowly to a stop, Rooster ran from behind the barn. He circled the van, yelping and barking. Gary said Rooster hadn't been acting like that, so somehow he must have sensed Randy was there.

When they lifted Randy from the van, Rooster rushed up to greet his master by licking him in the face. The small, spotted cowdog leapt and jumped around Randy until Randy reached out and scratched Rooster behind the ears.

While Randy was petting Rooster, he glanced around the grounds. It had been mid-winter the last time he had seen the place. Now it was summer and the property was all covered with high grass and weeds. He had always kept it mowed and neat, and it hurt him to see it like this.

"I thought you were taking care of the place, Gary."

"I try, but between working and rodeoing, it's hard."

Randy thought that he had better get home and take care of everything pretty soon, or there wouldn't be anything to take care of!

Gary and Press wheeled Randy into the horse barn so he could see Watch Joe and Ten. Both of the horses looked shaggy and unkempt to Randy. Ten was spooked by the wheelchair, but Watch Joe eased up to Randy. The curious horse stretched his neck to smell Randy and the weird-looking contraption underneath him. After sniffing Randy over well, he stood contentedly next to him.

Tears filled Randy's eyes as he slowly stroked Joe's side. Being home brought back all the memories of life before the accident. He thought his insides would burst. He desperately wanted to saddle Joe, ride off across the pasture and never look back... just keep riding until the memory of the past months was erased.

Randy decided that what he needed was a dip of snuff to cheer him up, so he asked Gary for one. Gary obliged. This proved to be a bad error in judgment, since Randy got sick immediately. He hurriedly spit the snuff out, but he was already turning green. This became a brilliant red, and that gave way to a pale white color.

Gary and Press went into a state of panic as they threw rather than lifted Randy into the van and sped off down the sandy lane toward the interstate and the hospital.

"You all right?" Gary asked, looking back at Randy as

they drove to the hospital.

"Man, I just thought I'd been sick before," Randy whispered weakly.

"Hang on, bud, we'll get you to the hospital in just a few minutes," Press said, increasing his speed.

"Hey man, don't you up and die on us... we wouldn't know where to take your body," Gary joked, attempting to lighten the mood.

When they lifted Randy out of the van and wheeled him to the second floor, Nancy was the first to see him.

"My Lord, what have you done to him?" she asked.

The two cowboys didn't reply. They looked almost as pale as Randy.

After that experience, Randy didn't have nerve enough to ask for another pass for a while.

Now, for the first time since the accident, Randy had a daily routine. He went to physical therapy in the mornings and occupational therapy in the afternoons. There were no set hours for visitation, so either family or friends were always visiting when he wasn't in therapy. It didn't seem as if there was a night someone wasn't with him.

The physical therapy was desperately needed. Before the accident he had worked out at least three to four times a week, bench-pressing three hundred pounds. After all, it took strong arms and shoulders to ride a bareback bronc. Mentally, he could still lift three hundred pounds, but physically, he could hardly lift his arm.

Randy looked forward to physical therapy but had no enthusiasm for occupational therapy or anything else not associated with his getting back the full use of his body. He told the therapist and occupational advisors that he didn't need to plan for a new career and a future in a wheelchair. He had a good job as a construction superintendent waiting for him. And he had a son to play with, horses to ride and rodeos to go to... that was his future. He didn't need to know how to do anything in a wheelchair because it was just a matter of time before he walked out of there and back into the life he had left... just as he had left it, standing upright.

Despite this, Randy began to have doubts when he seemed not to be making progress. But friends would visit and encourage him. One of those friends was Bob Lowe. Bob was a professional cowboy who rode bareback broncs. Riding barebacks was Randy's best rodeo event, so he felt a certain kinship with Bob. One day when Randy was desperately needing encouragement, Bob visited him.

"Bob, do you think I'll ever be able to rodeo again?" Randy asked.

"Sure. My brother was thrown from a bronc and broke his neck. They all told him he'd never walk again and would be paralyzed for the rest of his life. But he's back riding bareback horses. If he can do it, so can you."

"Where did he go for rehabilitation?" Randy asked, excited.

"Craig Institute in Colorado."

Randy knew that if he could just get to the Craig Institute, he would get better, and for weeks that was all he talked about.

It made Randy feel better just to hear about someone else making it back. It seemed all he heard from the hospital staff was that he needed to prepare himself for life in a wheelchair.

"Boy, I'd sure like to see a rodeo. I haven't seen a rodeo—

even on TV—since the accident," Randy commented.

"Well, by golly, we can sure fix that. I'll bring you a couple of rodeo videos. Of course they just happen to be the ones where I won," Bob said, grinning.

True to his word, Bob brought Randy two rodeo videos. As he lay there watching the rodeo action, Randy closed his eyes and imagined himself back riding. He could feel the exhilaration of sitting down on a twelve-hundred-pound bronc as the horse's muscles tightened and flexed in anticipation of the upcoming ride. He remembered how his heart would pump when he slipped the bareback rigging in place on the bronc's shoulder while another cowboy helped tighten the girth. He would stick his leather glove into the rigging's firm handle, working his right hand back and forth to warm the rosin rubbed into the glove. Rosin helped him grip the rigging handle. Once the chute gate flew open, it was just him and the bronc, so Randy needed all the strength he could muster. He would do his best to ride the bronc for eight seconds and the horse would do his best to buck Randy off.

Randy tensed as he mentally saw himself scoot up close to the rigging, placing both spurs at the point of the bronc's shoulders. Then, pulling hard on the rigging, he leaned back and called for the gate to be opened.

"Outside," he yelled out loud.

In Randy's vivid imagination, the bronc leapt high out of the chute while Randy leaned back and spurred. The bronc's head disappeared between his front legs and he leapt first to the left, then to the right, using every trick he knew. But Randy saw himself never losing control. Each time the bronc's feet hit the ground, it jarred every inch of Randy's body, but Randy stayed astraddle his back. Then the whistle blew, declaring the eight-second ride ended. Exhausted, Randy lay back against the pillow.

"What's going on in here?" Nancy asked as she entered the room.

"I just made a heck of a ride on a great bucking horse," he smiled.

"If you and that horse made a mess in here, you and that horse are goin' to clean it up," she replied, smiling. "Time for occupational therapy," she said cheerfully.

"That's a waste of time for them and me," Randy said, frowning.

"I don't say what's what around here. I just do what I'm told, and it's time for O.T. So, are you getting in that wheelchair by yourself, or you want help?"

"I'll do it myself."

Randy began the task of lowering himself from the bed into the wheelchair. Nancy knew better than to attempt to help him.

After several tries, Randy settled into the wheelchair.

"Nancy, I'm sorry I look and smell so bad," Randy said, frowning as he smelled himself.

"Look here, you're just like everyone else in this place, and you can't help it. Now I don't want to hear any more of that kind of talk," Nancy said, as she took hold of the wheelchair handles.

"I'm not everyone else," Randy replied, looking up at Nancy.

"I know you're not... and you just keep thinking like that."

Later that day, Randy tried weight lifting. His first attempt at weight lifting was devastating. He was able to lift only twenty-five pounds.

"I can't believe it," Randy said aloud, more to himself than the therapist standing next to him.

"You have to remember you have been on your back for four months. It'll take time to regain your strength," the tall, muscled therapist replied, as he folded his arms.

"I don't have time. I've already wasted too much time as it is," Randy answered, frowning.

He had always been an athlete who thrived on competition. It was simple and straightforward to Randy—if you wanted something badly enough, you just worked harder and longer until you achieved your goal. He remembered the motto they had used at the construction company: "Make it happen." That became his motto. When he got discouraged or when the pain became almost unbearable, he would think, "Make it happen."

Randy became obsessed with building himself back up physically without regard to his mental state. Other than occasional group encounters, he refused to have any contact with other paralyzed patients. He didn't have time to listen to their problems; he felt he had enough of his own. This was a complete reversal of Randy's character. Before the accident, he had been the first to visit sick and injured friends, and with his positive attitude and pleasant outlook on life, he had always been able to help cheer them up.

One of those people was Joe Mark Summers. Joe Mark had worked for the electric company and had been electrocuted while working on high voltage lines. He had received severe burns and other injuries that had resulted in his losing a leg to amputation. Joe Mark's mother had asked

Randy to talk with Joe, who had lost all desire to do anything but sit in a chair. Before the accident, Joe had been active in rodeo as a bull rider, and he and Randy had rodeoed together.

Randy would visit Joe Mark and encourage him to get on with his life. He was young and could still have a good, long, healthy life, Randy told him. Joe Mark's mother had told Randy that his visits helped.

One day Joe Mark appeared in the doorway of Randy's room.

"Hi, how you making out?" Joe Mark asked with a broad smile.

Randy had to look twice before he recognized him.

"Joe Mark?"

"Yep, in the flesh," he said as he pulled up a chair next to Randy.

"You're walking."

"Got a new leg," Joe Mark replied, holding up his leg to show Randy.

"That's great... so how're you doing?"

"Couldn't be better for a one-legged man. Don't do much bull riding, but manage most other things. Enough about me. How are you making out?"

"Making it," Randy said unconvincingly.

"Remember what you told me one time? You told me that my life wasn't over and that I needed to get on with it. Well, at the time I didn't want to hear that, but it made more of an impression than I thought. It must have, because here I am."

"I know what you're saying, Joe Mark, but I'm going to recover and I'm going to do everything I did before the accident. This is just temporary."

They talked for hours about rodeos, all the mutual friends they shared and who was doing what. Randy felt better just knowing that, after Joe Mark's severe injuries, he had made it back. Maybe there was hope after all.

When Joe Mark left, he laid a cane across the bed at Randy's feet.

"Here's something for you. Someday you'll use it."

"Thanks," Randy replied, smiling. But as soon as Joe Mark left the room, he wiggled around until he could grasp the cane and, with all the strength he had, threw it against the wall.

Randy was angry and frustrated. Sometimes he would think it was all just a terrible nightmare, that he would wake up and everything would be back to normal.

He became a regular at the physical therapy room, where he would push himself to exhaustion. Even Nancy suggested he slow down and give his body time to heal, but her advice went unheeded. It was clear to Randy what he had to do. He would read every book and article he could find on back injuries and would pay special attention to those where the patient had recovered.

Over the objections of his therapist, Randy convinced the staff to fashion leg braces from molded plastic and custom fit them to his legs. Randy had seen several patients walk out of Baylor with the aid of braces after having been brought in on a gurney. He was convinced that, if he could stand, it would just be a matter of time before he could walk.

Randy couldn't sleep the night before he was to try and walk with the braces. He barely touched breakfast and asked Nancy about every five minutes if it was time to go. Finally it was time, and Nancy rolled him to the third-floor therapy center.

"Randy, don't you go getting yourself too built up over those braces," Nancy said, as she pushed Randy into the elevator.

"I know it'll take time to walk normally, but the sooner I start, the sooner I'll be able to return to my life. I've got a son that needs me, horses to ride, and rodeos to go to. I don't have time for any of this."

"All I'm saying is, don't expect too much. It'll take time," Nancy replied.

When the elevator door opened, Randy felt as he had before each bronc ride: his stomach was tied in knots and his mouth felt as if it were full of cotton.

The braces had been carefully fitted, the straps tightened and checked. It was time to stand. He had been horizontal for months and the thought of standing made his heart feel as if it would leap out of his chest. Now, he would really begin recovery.

The staff wheeled Randy to the parallel bars and placed his feet on the floor.

"Are you ready?" the therapist asked.

"Yeah... open the gate," Randy managed a grin that went unnoticed by everyone except Nancy. She smiled.

Two muscled, white-clad men assisted Randy to his feet. Randy's pulse quickened, his head pounded and his stomach felt as if it were full of butterflies. He looked down at the floor. It seemed as if he were standing on a steel rail ten stories high, on top of one of the buildings he used to build. Then everything began to roll and move around.

"You all right?" the therapist asked.

"I think so," the bleary-eyed Randy replied weakly.

The floor seemed to be swaying, almost rolling like waves on an ocean. Randy felt the blood drain from his head... then blackness...

As Randy collapsed, the therapists caught him and carefully returned him to his wheelchair. Almost as quickly, Randy regained consciousness.

"What happened?" Randy asked, looking around.

"You fainted."

"Maybe you're not ready yet."

"Yes, I am," Randy said, as he straightened up.

Nancy bent over next to Randy and whispered: "Are you sure? Maybe it would be best to wait until tomorrow to try again."

"Nope, I can do it."

The only way they could convince Randy not to attempt standing again was to promise that they would help him stand the next day.

After he returned to his room, Randy stared at the ceiling in disbelief. How was he going to walk when he couldn't even stand up? He had just known he was going to be able to stand and walk. But instead of walking, he had passed out like some kind of a weakling sissy.

About that time, James walked in.

"I hear you stood up," James said cheerfully.

"I dropped like a sick fly," Randy replied disgustedly.

"Hey man, you stood up—that's a start. Just keep in mind that a few months ago they said you wouldn't make it through seventy-two hours. You've already beat the odds."

"I just want to get back to normal and get on with my life."

"Remember the motto?" James asked.

"Make it happen," Randy said.

"You got it," James replied, smiling.

The next day, Randy was more nervous than he had been the day before. Instead of putting braces on Randy, the therapists strapped him onto a tilt table. This would help him slowly get used to being erect.

"I feel like Frankenstein, strapped on this dang thing," Randy commented.

"We're going to tilt you a little at a time until you're upright," the therapist said.

Randy was able to tolerate being completely vertical, but he was more light-headed than he let on. He had found out the hard way that every setback meant staying an additional month. So he just smiled and told them he was fine.

After several days on the tilt table, Randy was able to stand with the aid of the special braces and the support of a podium-like structure. Everything looked different from a standing position!

Randy continued physical therapy and weight lifting to regain his upper-body strength, looking forward to the day he could walk unassisted.

After a few days of standing, he convinced his therapist to let him try walking while holding onto the parallel bars. The therapist, tired of arguing with Randy, consented.

Randy was wheeled up to the two, ten-foot-long parallel bars. He glanced first to the left bar, then to the right, then straight ahead. The ten feet to the other end looked like an endless tunnel. His heart pounded in anticipation as he lifted one leg, then the other, from his chair. The braces were fitted and carefully strapped into the proper position... it was time. Randy swallowed, briefly wondering why his mouth was so dry. Then he held his arms up so he could be assisted to his feet.

He stood holding onto the bars as both therapists loosened their grip on Randy's arms and moved back. Randy glanced first left, then right, to make sure no one was helping him. He looked straight ahead once more, judging the distance. "Well," he thought to himself, "this is it. Can I walk or not?" He intensified his grip on the bars, gritted his teeth, and whispered out loud, "Make it happen." Then he strained with all his might to make his right foot move forward. Nothing... Again... Nothing. His face and neck turned red from straining and his shoulders began to shake from holding his weight up. "Make it happen," he repeated out loud. As his exhausted arms began to slowly collapse, the therapists rushed to grab him before he fell.

Randy was quiet when Nancy wheeled him back to his room. He had failed. Not only had he failed the people who believed in him, he had failed himself.

That night Randy felt more alone and desperate than he had since the night of his accident. He prayed to God for guidance, but never felt His presence. Thinking God had deserted him, he finally drifted off into an uneasy, fitful sleep.

The next day, the hospital staff moved a paraplegic patient named Michael into the room with Randy. Michael had been paralyzed by a skiing accident seventeen years earlier and he was being treated for pressure sores. He was from California and had been visiting his brother, who lived in Dallas.

His injuries were similar to Randy's and he sensed Randy's pain and frustration. After his accident, Michael had gone through the same feelings Randy was experiencing now, and so he tried to help him.

"Randy, you've got to forget about walking and get on with your life. Your life is not over, but you have to make it sitting rather than standing," Michael said, turning to face Randy.

"Look, I don't need someone else telling me I can't do something. There's plenty of doctors and nurses and therapists telling me I can't walk," Randy replied bitterly.

"Yeah, but they're not paralyzed... I am. And I'm telling you for your own good: get on with your life!"

Randy hated Michael for what he had said. It was one thing to hear it from walking people, but it sounded too real and final from someone like himself.

"You don't know me or anything about me," Randy said. "My injuries are different from yours."

"No, they're not, and deep down inside, you know that."

Randy never changed his position during the two weeks Michael was his roommate. But the words Michael had spoken haunted him night and day.

When he went to therapy, Randy attacked the weights as if they were his enemy. He spent every waking hour in the physical therapy room, pulling and lifting. When he had participated in sports as a young man and hadn't performed as he thought he should, he had just worked harder and longer. This had been his normal approach, and he used it again now. Work harder... longer... make it happen.

He finally got to the point where he could lift his legs, and shuffle them forward while holding onto the parallel bars and flexing his shoulders. He was able to shuffle first the left, then the right leg, and, in a hopping gait, manage to go the length of the parallel bars. Randy was fooling himself into believing he was walking.

He even attempted to walk on a treadmill, thinking that his legs had forgotten how to move, and all they needed was a reminder. But they never remembered.

One night about nine o'clock, after he had been at Baylor for four months, a determined Randy socked his black, wide-brimmed cowboy hat on his head. He went to the physical therapy room by himself, after stopping by the nurses' station and telling them where he was going.

As the elevator door opened onto the physical therapy floor, the smell reminded Randy of the school gym where he had worked out as a kid. He wheeled himself up to the pull weights and locked the wheels on his wheelchair. He pulled the handles, and the attached weights moved easily as he flexed his arms. Anger began to build as he pulled the handles in an even motion. Gritting his teeth, he pulled harder. Tears filled his eyes as he violently jerked the handles first on one side, then the other. In complete frustration, he then threw the handles as hard as he could. The cables immediately retracted and the weights slammed against the floor. Then all was quiet.

"Lord, I'm beaten. Why have you forsaken me?" Randy sobbed uncontrollably.

The elevator opened and Gary Mitchell stepped out. Seeing Randy slumped down in his chair, he hurried over to him.

"You all right?" Gary asked, laying his hand on Randy's shoulder.

Randy looked up at his friend through tear-blurred eyes. "I'm not ever going to walk again."

"That's not true. You will walk again."

Gary squatted down next to Randy and put his arm over his shoulder.

"You can't talk like that. It's up to the Lord, not the doctors and nurses. Now, no more of that stuff about not walking... OK?" Gary whispered.

"No, Gary, I'm not ever going to walk again. And I've got to face it."

Now he had said out loud what he had been thinking to himself for weeks. He held his head between his hands and sobbed uncontrollably. Gary encircled his friend with both arms as tears ran down Randy's cheeks.

"You're going to make it," he repeated over and over as they huddled together.

Randy spent a restless night after Gary left. He desperately needed answers so he looked to God for guidance. Sometime during the night, his prayers were answered. He awoke with a feeling of contentment, a feeling he had not experienced in many months. It was the same exhilarating, content feeling he had had when Brett was born. As he lay in bed staring at the ceiling, the feeling became a vision. It was simple. God had not forsaken him, for in God's eyes, he was healed. Randy was healed of the need to be healed. For now, it was God's will that Randy not walk. There were more important things for him to accomplish, and those accomplishments would be from a wheelchair.

Chapter 7

Randy's attitude toward occupational therapy changed drastically overnight. The hospital staff wondered what had prompted the complete turnaround, but he never told anyone other than his immediate family and Nancy what had happened.

He began learning how to use a wheelchair as he did everything, with complete enthusiasm and dedication. He immediately began making suggestions to improve wheelchairs and began questioning the staff's methods and procedures. At times the instructors and therapists wished he were more like he had been before.

Without having to waste energy thinking about walking, Randy focused on regaining his health and becoming proficient in caring for himself in a wheelchair. He learned how to cook, shower, jump curbs, load and unload his wheelchair, and all the other things a paralyzed person has to know to survive day-to-day living.

Since he had no control over his bodily excretions, he learned how to catheterize himself and clean himself after bowel movements. Taking a shower without assistance took an hour, and that was with shower facilities specially designed for the disabled. Things that Randy had accepted as minor routines before the accident became major tasks. He learned early on that he had to be extra clean and sterile in his procedures because of the threat of infections. He had to be constantly aware of the potential for deadly bladder infections.

How he was going to make a living for himself and support Brett were two things always on Randy's mind. He couldn't see himself sitting indoors all day at some desk job; he had been outdoors all his life. And even though he knew there was no way he could compete in rough stock rodeo events, he wanted to participate in some capacity. He just had to think it through and come up with solutions. It was evident he couldn't return to his construction job. It would be a little difficult to walk the beams of a high-rise building in a wheelchair! So he began considering options.

Pa decided that Randy needed to think about things other than physical and occupational therapy, so he told Randy about a place he had located. He wanted Randy to go in with him—lease the place, buy some cows and raise a few calves. Now Pa didn't really care about cows; he just wanted Randy to have something to look forward to and think about.

After the two agreed to go in as partners, Pa leased the place and arranged to have Randy go with him to look at some cows that were for sale. Randy got a day pass, and Pa picked him up one morning in late summer.

It was already hot by the time they pulled into the cow lot. Pa pulled the car to where Randy could see the cows they were considering buying. Before leaving, the two made a deal to buy the ones they had selected, and Pa made arrangements to have the cows trailered to the lease property.

Randy and Pa were now officially in the cow business. This was another of Pa's own "treatments," of which there were many.

Randy knew he had to learn how to make it on his own. James still made the trip from the coast on a regular basis, and he and Randy began making plans for James and Becky to move their family closer.

They planned on moving into their mother's house, since she and her husband, Bill, were in Oklahoma City. The house was next door to Pa's and Nanny's. After Randy had completely recovered and was capable of making it on his own, he could move back to his ranch house.

Randy stayed busy, lifting weights, going to occupational and range-of-motion therapy sessions where they would stretch his legs and move his ankle and knee joints. He still had no feeling at all below his chest. His days began early and ended with him in the weight room late in the evening by himself. It was apparent he had to develop upper-body strength, since everything he did involved lifting or turning himself. Without leg strength, the ability to lift himself had to come from his arms and shoulders. He liked to work out at night when no one was there, since then he could think more clearly without distraction and stay focused.

Randy began thinking about things outside of the hospital, things that required attention—his attention. He was beginning to feel as if he had regained some control over his life. He thought about the horses. He decided he would keep Ten and Watch Joe and a few of the better mares, but everything else needed to be sold. There would be some income from the colts produced, and he could breed the mares back to Ten. There was opportunity for additional income if he bred a few outside mares to Ten, but he needed to get Ten out where the public could see him. And the best way to do that would be to show him at cutting.

One morning when he knew James was coming to visit, Randy decided to ask his brother about riding and showing Ten at cutting. The young stallion badly needed cutting work—no one had used him for cutting since the day before the accident. Gary was riding him and trying to keep the horse in shape, but he didn't have time to take him to cuttings. It was Randy's plan to show James how he rode Ten, and get James to take Ten to practice cutting. So when James walked in, Randy was ready.

"How are you doing?" James asked, as he walked in and sat down next to Randy in his wheelchair.

"Good. How's the family?"

"Everyone's OK. Seen Mama and Pa yet today?"

"Mama's back in Oklahoma City for a while, but Pa will be here after a while."

"Good."

"How about you taking Ten to some practice cuttings?" Randy asked.

"I'm no cutter. Isn't Gary riding him?"

"Yeah, but he doesn't have time to haul him around. Besides, he's not a cutter."

"Well... I'll try, but I don't have a lot of time."

"I can get a couple of day passes and show you how I rode him. If we ride him alike, maybe it won't mess him up. What do you think?" Randy asked.

"I'll give it a try."

Randy felt better. But now he needed someone to ride Watch Joe until he could.

James rode Ten for several months, taking him to cuttings while Randy watched and offered suggestions. It wasn't like riding Ten himself, but it beat sitting in the hospital.

Randy and James spent much of their time together planning things they were going to do once Randy was released from the hospital. They talked about *how* Randy would be able to ride a horse, not *if*. In their minds, they would find a way. The first thing Randy was going to do was get a truck—a cowboy has to have transportation. Then Brett and he would drive around the countryside looking at crops growing in the fields, and cows and horses grazing in green pastures. They would just sit in the sun with a warm breeze blowing through the open windows. Randy wanted to experience the things that make a person know he is alive. He wanted to sit and talk with Brett, it didn't matter about what. He never wanted to be shut in again... never again in his life.

Randy continued to have a steady stream of visitors and, even though he was glad to see them, it took him away from his routine. So that he could visit and still accomplish something positive toward recovery, he began keeping dumbbells in his room. That way he could lift the weights while talking to his company.

Randy enjoyed all his friends and visitors but he looked forward most to the visits from his close cowboy friends. Cowboys are a strange bunch in a lot of ways, but when a fellow cowboy is hurting or down and out, they are there to help.

One of the many visitors was Butch Green, a team roper Randy had roped with on occasion.

"Hey, Randy," Butch said, smiling, as he entered Randy's room.

"Come on in, Butch, and sit. What in the world have you been up to?" Randy said, extending his hand.

"Not a whole lot. Just working and roping a few steers now and again."

"How you doing?" Butch asked.

"Making it."

"When do you think you'll be out and about?" Butch asked.

"I'm hoping to go home in a few weeks."

It was evident to Butch that Randy wasn't going to walk out of the hospital as Randy had anticipated when he first came to Baylor.

"How's therapy going?"

"It's going somewhat better than it was, but I've still got a long way to go. I've got to where I can press eighty pounds—that's a little down from the 315 I pressed before the accident," Randy said.

Butch wasn't sure just what to say. They stared at the floor in silence for several minutes.

"Butch, I'm not going to walk, at least not right now. The Lord apparently has more use for me in a wheelchair. If there comes a time when I'll be more useful to Him standing and walking, then I will," Randy said, breaking the silence.

"Let me tell you about something that happened to me one time," Butch interrupted. "I was at a rodeo and got thrown hard off a bareback bronc. I jammed my neck pretty good, and it hurt like hell. You know how it is—at a rodeo you're pretty well on your own. So I drove myself to the nearest hospital, walked into the emergency room and told them what had happened. They took some X-rays and determined that my neck was broken. I spent a bunch of time in a body cast and with one of those halo things screwed into my skull. I was in a hell of a mess, but now here I am walking and talking and still riding."

"I never knew that," Randy said.

"Never came up before," Butch replied.

Randy knew that Butch was just trying to encourage him. But like most of the cowboys who had visited him, Butch didn't understand the extent of Randy's injuries. Fractured and depressed vertebra were one thing, but bone fragments in the spinal column were something altogether different.

"I know what you're saying, Butch, but the fact of the matter is, I'm not going to walk out of here like I said in the beginning," Randy said, as tears began to slowly run down his cheek.

"Damn it, Randy... it ain't right," Butch said, as he put his arm over Randy's shoulder. "It ain't right," he cried.

Gary Mitchell flashed into view through the open doorway, and like a thief in the night, he stepped quickly into the room. He grasped a nylon bag with one hand and quietly shut the door.

"What are you up to?" Randy asked. It had been a rough night, and he welcomed anything that would erase the lingering bad memories. He had started having nightmares about the accident almost a month earlier, and they had recurred three or four times a week since then.

Gary held his hand up in a gesture of silence. Then he

pulled the sheets back, exposing Randy's legs.

"Come on, Gary. What are you doing?" Without answering, Gary spread Randy's legs and reached into the nylon bag. He pulled out Randy's old rodeo bareback rigging and stuck it between his legs in a riding position as if it were on a bronc.

Randy started to reach for the rigging handle and Gary put his hand up again to protest any movement. He reached into the bag one more time and handed Randy his old riding glove. The leather glove was discolored from several coats of rosin and sweat from Randy and the many broncs he had ridden. It had a distinct odor.

Gary held the glove up to Randy's nose. "Ain't that about the best smelling thing you ever smelled?" Gary whispered.

Randy took a deep breath. The aroma of leather and horse filled his senses, and, for a brief moment, he was back on the bucking chute waiting his turn to ride.

"Put it on, cowboy," Gary insisted. Randy slipped the hard, leather glove on his right hand and slowly but deliberately worked his hand into the firm rigging handle placed between his legs.

"Well, cowboy... you goin' to stay in the chute, or are you going to spur this ol' bronc out?" Gary asked, backing away from the bed.

Randy tightened his grip, pulled back on the rigging and closed his eyes. In his imagination he was back on a bronc. Randy nodded his head, signaling that he was ready to begin the ride.

Almost instantly, Randy opened his tear-filled eyes and glanced down at the rigging between his thin, motionless legs. The only broncs he would ever ride again would be in his imagination. He felt sick to his stomach.

"Well, it seemed like a good idea at the time," Gary said softly.

"Hey, I appreciate it. I don't know what's got into me. I reckon I'm just feeling sorry for myself," Randy replied, wiping the tears away.

They were both silent.

Randy pulled the glove off and handed the rigging to Gary.

"Thanks, buddy, I really do appreciate it."

"You bet, glad to do it," Gary answered as he shoved the rigging and glove into the nylon bag.

"How are the horses doing?" Randy asked, breaking the silence.

"They're doing all right, I suppose. They get fed twice a day—that's more than I get fed most the time," Gary remarked, smiling.

"Winning any rodeos?" Randy asked.

"Every once in a while. Just enough to make me keep going. If I was to quit winning altogether, maybe I'd quit rodeoing."

"Never happen."

"Well, got stuff to do. See you in a couple of days," Gary said as he zipped the rigging bag and headed towards the door.

"Hey, leave the bag," Randy said, holding his hand out.

"Is it allowed?"

"It is if they don't know about it. Gary, thanks again. I'm going to make it somehow."

"Never doubted it," Gary said as he opened the door and disappeared into the hallway.

As Randy's physical condition improved, so did his mental attitude. He began to visit with other patients, offering them encouragement and a sympathetic ear. He could relate to them in a way that the hospital staff couldn't. Randy had been there. He knew how they felt. He knew what their fears were. He knew, because he still had those fears himself: the fear of the unknown, of helplessness, of dependency on others, and most of all, of loss of control over the basic things in life. But by helping others suppress their fears, Randy was helping himself to do the same. Sometimes, he found, you learn by teaching.

It became a daily routine for Randy to visit patients throughout the hospital, going from room to room. Sometimes he would sit for hours holding the hand of a child who wasn't even aware that Randy was there. It was hard to see anyone injured severely, but to see a child in that condition was devastating. Randy had always been compassionate, but now, after seeing so many people with such terrible injuries, he developed compassion and love such as he had never thought possible. One thing he was now sure of—whatever he did with the rest of his life, it would include helping people wherever and whenever he could. And he would never be a bargaining Christian again. He would offer his testimony to Christ at every opportunity and become the Christian he had always believed he was.

Randy also became more aware of the simple things in life—a child's smile or laugh, sunrise and sunset, and the company of a friend. Randy was healing both physically and emotionally, and in the process finding out who he really was and what he could be.

With his black cowboy hat socked down on his head and

wearing green hospital garb, Randy became a familiar sight throughout the hospital. James brought him a lariat rope, and Randy roped everything and everyone in sight.

There were incidents that almost got Randy released prematurely, like the time two of Randy's cowboy friends were pushing him down the halls at a run, jerking and rearing the wheelchair as Randy bounced side to side shouting "Ride him, cowboy." Then there was the time they decided to have a roping contest, using Randy's wheelchair as the steer. They brought guitars and sang, and talked about horses and rodeos for hours. It was great therapy for Randy, but sometimes disturbing to the hospital staff.

After he had been at Baylor for almost six months, Randy decided it was time for him to go home. He had been asking for several weeks when he would be able to leave, but to no avail. Now he was going to tell them that it was time.

After a lot of argument and discussion with doctors and therapists, it was decided he would be released within the week. Randy spent the next few days visiting all the other patients, telling them he would be back to visit, a promise he still keeps to this day.

The toughest thing of all was telling Nancy goodbye. She had seen him through some of his worst times and had never treated him like just another paralyzed patient. Nancy cared about her patients. They weren't just a name and room number. Randy would miss her.

Eight months after being admitted to Methodist Hospital, Randy was released on February 24, 1986.

Chapter 8

It was a beautiful early fall day as James pushed Randy down the cement ramp to the waiting car. Randy's mind whirled with thoughts about the past and the uncertain future.

He thought about the challenges he would face in a world designed and built for normal people, people without physical disabilities. He remembered how people had reacted the few times he had ventured out in public on day passes. They had stared when he had attempted to jump curbs because there wasn't a ramp for wheelchair access, or when he had struggled to open an oversized, heavy door. Mostly people were hesitant to offer assistance; many would just walk away quickly or ignore him altogether. It was as if they felt that, if they didn't acknowledge his presence, they wouldn't have to deal with him.

Here at Baylor, Randy had received many hours of instructions on handling life in a wheelchair, but he thought he would need just as many hours of instructions on coping with other people's attitudes and lack of empathy toward the disabled. He realized there were changes that would have to be made to support the growing number of physically challenged persons, and that those changes would have to start with the disabled.

Randy asked James to stop and turn him around. There were several staff members and patients in wheelchairs still lingering on the second-floor balcony, watching him leave. He waved and smiled.

"I'll be back. I won't forget you. I'll never forget any of you," Randy said, knowing they couldn't hear him.

They waved back as James turned him around.

Randy was physically and mentally exhausted by the time he arrived at his mother's house and settled in. James, his wife, Becky, and their two children had moved from the coast the week before and had everything ready.

Up until now Randy had used facilities designed and built for the physically disabled. Now he would have to make do with facilities built for able-bodied people.

Randy, Pa, and James planned out how to fix things around the house to make it a little easier for Randy. They bought a small, straight chair that would fit in the bathtub, so Randy could sit while he showered. Everything that he needed on a daily basis was lowered to within his reach or made accessible in other ways. Most of the door openings were wide enough for him to pass through with his wheelchair, and he could reach all the light switches.

Pa, and James had brought his clothes, weights and personal things from the ranch the day before, and they set his weights up in the garage for his daily workouts.

It was apparent he had to build up his upper-body strength.

For the first time in eight months, he did things when he wanted. It was a good feeling. He was still plagued with infections that weakened him and left him sick at his stomach much of the time, but at least he was out of the hospital.

After a few days of trial and error, everyone settled into a routine. Randy would wait until James' kids, Amy and Cody, were ready for school. Then he would take his shower and shave. In the beginning, he would take his clothes off on the bed, and James would push him next to the bathtub in his wheelchair. Then James would lift Randy from the wheelchair to the chair set up in the bathtub. Randy still didn't have the strength to lift himself. Then James would turn on the shower and help Randy bathe.

Afterwards Randy would catheterize himself and dress, but he needed help getting his boots on and off.

By the time a couple of weeks had passed, he decided that it was time to get a truck. He had been checking the car advertisements in the local newspaper and had found a truck he wanted to look at, so he asked Pa to take him. Randy knew there was a place in Dallas that installed hand-operated brake and accelerator systems on vehicles. He planned to pick out the truck he wanted and have someone drive it to Dallas to have the systems installed.

Pa pulled into the driveway. Randy wheeled himself to the car and opened the door.

"Watch this," Randy said, as he struggled to lift himself from the wheelchair to the car seat.

"Can I help?" Pa asked.

"Nope, I'll make it."

James' wife, Becky, came out of the house and hurried to Randy's side as he struggled to lift himself from the wheelchair.

"Here, let me help you," Becky said, positioning herself to help lift him.

"No, thanks, Becky. You do everything for me as it is. I've got to learn how to do things on my own."

Becky moved back, obviously hurt. All she had wanted to do was help. "I'm sorry," she said.

After several attempts, Randy was able to lift himself from the wheelchair and wiggle onto the car seat. Out of breath and weak, he smiled at Pa.

"Made it."

Randy turned and waved to Becky as Pa backed out of the driveway.

"Kind of hard on Becky, weren't you?" Pa commented.

"Becky is smothering me. I know all she wants to do is help, but I've got to do for myself or I'll never be on my own," Randy replied.

They looked over the new trucks at the car dealership in Rockwall. Randy found the one he wanted, and a deal was made. Randy was too excited to wait for someone to drive the truck to Dallas, so he told Pa he would drive it home himself. Besides, he didn't want anyone else putting the first miles on his new truck. That treat should be reserved for him. When Randy told Pa what he was going to do, Pa looked at him in disbelief.

"You're going to do what?"

"I'm going to drive the truck home."

"How do you plan on doing that?"

"You remember that walking cane Joe Mark gave me?"

"Yes, but what does that have to do with you driving?"

"Take me home and I'll show you."

Randy told the salesman to have his truck ready in an

hour and he would be back to get it.

The round trip to the house took about an hour. By the time they returned, the truck was cleaned up and parked beside the building, ready to go.

The salesman walked out to meet them as Pa pulled up next to the truck.

"Randy, don't you think it would be better if we waited for James? Or Becky could drive it home," Pa said.

"Nope, I can do it," Randy replied, opening the car door.

Pa came around to the passenger side and asked Randy what he needed him to do.

"If you and he," Randy said, pointing to the salesman, "could just sit me behind the steering wheel, I'll take it from there."

"Is he going to drive?" the salesman asked, glancing at Pa as they lifted Randy into the truck cab.

"Says he is," Pa replied.

Randy adjusted the seat and pulled the seat belt tight over his shoulder and around his waist. Then he started the engine.

"Boy, don't that sound good?" he asked, smiling.

Pa and the salesman stood watching in disbelief as Randy pulled the door shut and rolled down the window.

"Hand me that walking cane, Pa. I'm going to walk this truck on home," he said smiling.

Pa handed him the cane through the window and backed away.

Randy held the cane with his right hand. By extending it to the floor, he was able to push down on the accelerator and brake and apply enough pressure to accelerate or stop the truck. He slipped the truck into reverse and backed up.

Then he pulled it forward a few times until he got the feel of it. As he glanced toward the interstate service road, however, his mouth suddenly became very dry and sweat popped out on his forehead.

"OK, Randy. You've been waiting for this day for a long time. Don't freeze up now," Randy thought to himself.

It was one thing to talk about being on his own, but it was something else altogether to actually be by himself.

Forcing himself to smile, he glanced at Pa.

"Ready?" he asked, his voice strained.

"If you are. Are you sure you want to do this?" Pa asked, clearly concerned.

"You bet, no problem," Randy replied, not feeling as confident as he sounded.

Pa hurried back to his car as the salesman watched in disbelief.

Randy slowly pulled onto the interstate access road. It had been a long time since he had driven, and the last time he had ended up in a ditch. He slowly pushed down on the accelerator with his cane and the truck responded. When he applied more pressure with the extended walking cane and the truck picked up speed, his heart started pounding. After all these months he was finally free! He was taking control of his life and it was exhilarating. But at the same time it was terrifying. What if he couldn't stop? What if he lost control? What if he hit loose gravel? He could end up back in the hospital, or maybe dead. He knew he had to stop thinking about those things. He had to take it one step at a time.

He eased to a stop by pushing down on the brake pedal with the cane. After a few stops and turns, he felt more comfortable with the arrangement. He smiled when he thought about Joe Mark giving him the cane and telling him he would need it someday. Well, that day had come, but he didn't believe Joe Mark had thought it would be used this way.

It was several days before the truck could be equipped, so Randy drove around using the cane. He attempted to pull himself into the seat, but he was still too weak, so he had to depend on someone to help him.

Whenever he started thinking about all the things that could happen to him by himself he would begin to panic. What if he had a flat tire? What if the truck quit running? If he were stranded on a country road, it could be hours or days before someone happened along and found him.

As the panic rose, Randy would turn the radio volume up and sing along with the tune until the fear subsided. He kept telling himself he could handle the situation, whatever it was. Eventually, he made it home.

From then on, he forced himself to drive every day, taking short trips to check on the cows. He would drive to the cow pasture, turn the engine off and sit there as long as he could.

He remembered the therapist telling him not to sit in one position too long, and not to bump himself hard. All these things could cause pressure sores. After what he had gone through with pressure sores in the hospital, he didn't ever want to have another one, so he was careful.

Things were beginning to settle into a routine. Brett visited almost every weekend, but that wasn't enough for

Randy. He wanted Brett to be with him all the time. Randy and Donna, Brett's mother, had heated discussions about Brett coming to live with Randy, but the issue was never resolved.

Then one morning Donna called Randy and told him she wanted to talk later that day. Randy told her to come any time she wanted, since he wasn't going anywhere.

Later that day, Donna pulled in the driveway and came to the door. Becky invited her in, and, sensing that it was to be a private conversation, excused herself and left the room.

"Randy, I have made a decision," Donna said. She hesitated, not sure she wanted to continue. "I have decided that you need Brett." She hesitated again, tears filling her eyes, "and he needs you, so I am willing to let him live with you," she said softly, looking down.

Randy couldn't believe what he was hearing! It had been a dream of his for years to have Brett with him. His heart pounded as he looked at Donna.

"Are you sure?" he asked.

"No, and you'd better just say OK, or I might change my mind," she said, looking at Randy.

"OK, I don't know how to thank you."

"I'll think of something," Donna said, smiling.

Then she stood up and walked over to Randy, put her arms around him and held him tight.

"Thank you from the bottom of my heart," Randy whispered, tears running down his face.

"I'll bring Brett this weekend. You'll have to get him enrolled at Royse City School next week," she said, as she walked through the door, not looking back.

From that day on, Brett was his father's constant

companion. Small as Brett was, he helped his father struggle into the truck cab. They drove the back roads together, checking the cows. They even began taking limited care of the horses at the ranch. It was beginning to be as Randy had dreamed in the hospital—he and Brett together, making a life for themselves.

Randy never forgot his vow to God about not being a bargaining Christian. He offered daily prayers for the many blessings he had received. He thanked the Lord for giving him his life back, for the support of his family and friends, but most of all for Brett, and for Donna's unselfish decision to let Brett live with him. It had taken outstanding courage and love to do what she had done.

Some time after Brett came to live with him, Randy heard about the Dallas Rehabilitation Institute. He began thinking that, maybe with the new state-of-the-art electronic therapy equipment they had, the institute staff might be able to help him.

He contacted the institute and made an appointment for an evaluation the following Monday morning. It was hard not to be excited over the possibilities, but at the same time he had to try to be realistic.

When he arrived at the institute, Randy was impressed with the people and the facility. Maybe this was the place that would help him walk.

He had taken his X-rays and medical records with him, hoping that with all the advances being made in electronic stimulation, they would be able to get some movement back in his legs. If he could once get movement, he knew he could walk.

But after many hours of evaluation and tests, it was determined that the nerves in Randy's legs could not be stimulated. The highest electrical pulsing charge was used, without response. He was considered to have no reflex arc. The staff finally recommended that Randy concentrate on building up his upper-body strength.

It was hard for Randy to accept their findings. He had convinced himself that this was the time he would be healed and would recover completely. But it was not to be.

But, although he had to resign himself all over again to the idea of never walking, Randy still enjoyed his connection with the institute. One of several people Randy met there was Kristi Koonsman. Kristi, a teenager who lived in Hico, Texas, came from a ranching family. She had ridden horses all her life, so she and Randy shared a common love for ranch life and horses. Like Randy, she had hoped for complete recovery after falling out of a tree and breaking her back. But, also like Randy, she wasn't given any encouragement.

Continuing as an outpatient for two months, Randy attended sessions two or three times a week and began to build up his upper body. He was introduced to a Hydraflex machine and was so impressed with it that he bought one from the manufacturer to have at home.

Infections still recurred frequently. Bladder infections would drain Randy of his strength and cause him to delay his exercise program. He blamed the infections on his daily catheterization. No matter how he scrubbed and took precautions, the infections persisted.

Randy had been regularly sending urine samples to Doctors Hospital in Dallas for analysis. Early one Monday morning he received a call from the hospital that he needed to check in for additional testing. Randy had committed himself to giving his testimony at a church in Greenville that Wednesday night and told the nurse he couldn't come to the hospital until after that.

About ten minutes later, a doctor called, telling Randy that he had to be tested and treated immediately. The bladder infection he had could be life-threatening. Randy explained again that he had made a commitment to give his testimony Wednesday and that he would not break that commitment. But, he told the doctor, he would check into the hospital if he could have a pass to leave long enough to give his testimony. The doctor agreed and Randy checked into the hospital before noon on Monday.

By Wednesday, Randy was weak and sick from the infection. But that evening Becky still picked him up at the hospital and drove him to the church where the rest of Randy's family was already waiting.

Randy was relieved when he noticed there were only a few cars in the parking lot. With the infection—combined with the excitement of speaking before a crowd of people— he was feeling sicker and sicker.

Pa pushed Randy into the church and down to the front.

"Pa, I don't know what to say," Randy whispered, turning his head so he could see Pa.

"Don't worry about it. God will tell you what to say."

"I sure hope so... because right now I don't have any ideas."

After Randy talked with his family and the minister for a few minutes, they lifted him onto the stage and sat him facing the congregation. The last time he had glanced around, there had been only a few people sitting scattered about. But now the church was filled to capacity! There were people sitting in the aisles and standing in the back.

Randy's heart felt as if it would jump out of his chest. He thought he had done it now. When he had committed to give his testimony, it had seemed so simple. Now, faced with so many people sitting out there looking at him, he was scared to death. He didn't have any idea what to say. While the service was in progress, Randy didn't hear a word that was spoken until the minister introduced him.

"I want to introduce Randy Bird," the minister said, turning to face Randy. "Randy will give his testimony to Christ tonight, and God will use him like he has never been used before."

Randy closed his eyes and prayed.

"Dear Jesus, help me."

Then he slowly wheeled himself up to the microphone. He had never been so nervous in his life.

"Well... I guess it's my turn," he said, smiling.

Randy spoke for one hour describing the accident, quoting applicable scriptures from the Bible as he talked. The remarkable thing was, he didn't know what he had said until he heard a taped recording later.

The congregation did indeed receive a blessing that Wednesday night. And God did use Randy Bird as he had never been used before.

More than six hundred worshippers attended the service that Wednesday night and all of them were truly affected by the words of a young paralyzed cowboy who, only a short two hours earlier, hadn't known what to say.

Randy returned to the hospital that night and tests were

run until the following week.

It was decided that his bladder was healthy and the infections were mostly due to a breakdown in his immune system. He was given a strong antibiotic to help fight the infections until his own body was strong enough to take over.

After returning from the hospital, Randy decided he and Brett should be living at the ranch. They made plans to relocate as soon as possible.

Randy drove over to the ranch one Saturday morning to tell Gary they would be moving. He wanted to give Gary as much time as he could. Randy pulled up in front of the ranch house and honked the horn. Gary appeared at the door and waved.

"Be there in a minute," he shouted.

Randy turned the radio on, and, as he waited for Gary, looked around the grounds. "One of the first things I've got to do is rig the tractor up so I can drive it," he thought. "Then I've got to get this place back into shape. Maybe I'll have time to get winter wheat or oats planted before Thanksgiving. That will at least give the stock something green to graze on this winter and early spring."

Gary knocked on the door, startling Randy.

"Thought you went to sleep," Gary said, opening the truck door. "What's going on?"

"Not much, just thought I'd drop over," Randy replied.

"You've got something on your mind. What is it?"

"Looks like we'll be moving back home in the next week or so. Just wanted to let you know, and tell you how much I appreciate you looking out for things while I was gone."

"I figured you would be moving back pretty soon. Are your brother and his family moving, too?"

"Yeah, at least for a while."

"Well, I believe I'll head on back to Alabama for a while."

"I was hoping you'd stay around here."

"Oh, I'll be back for sure next spring. Got to make all these big-money Texas rodeos," he smiled.

"James and Pa need to build a ramp and make a few modifications to the house before we move. Will that cause you a problem?"

"Shoot, no."

"Don't take off without saying goodbye," Randy said, looking at his friend. "You've been a good friend, Gary, and I'll sure miss you."

"Hey, I'm just going to Alabama. It ain't like I'm leaving the country or something."

Before Randy moved back, Pa and James built a ramp from the house to a concrete walkway. This allowed Randy to park his truck next to the cement walk, unload his wheelchair beside his truck, slide onto his wheelchair and wheel himself to the house unassisted. They also made modifications to the bathroom, enlarging the door opening and plumbing in an extended, hand-held shower head. Additional modifications to make daily life even more convenient came later.

Gary left the day they moved in, and it affected Randy even more than he had thought it would. Gary had been there for him when he desperately needed someone, and it was something not easily forgotten. Gary Mitchell would be missed.

Chapter 9

The day before moving to the ranch, Randy developed yet another infection that left him sick and weak. The illnesses seemed to follow a cycle. He would begin to make progress in building up his strength and gaining weight, then he would lose it all. He still didn't weigh much over one hundred pounds.

The day after moving, Randy was lying in bed, looking out the window. Watch Joe was standing in a corral next to the barn, and Randy had an overwhelming urge to ride him.

"James," Randy shouted.

"Yeah," James replied, opening the bedroom door.

"Would you saddle Watch Joe? I want to ride him."

"I will if you want me to, but shouldn't you wait until you feel better?"

"I'm not waiting another day. It's time," Randy said, determined.

It took James a few minutes to catch and saddle Watch Joe. The horse hadn't been ridden since before Randy's accident, and he was feeling frisky and snorty. James led the sorrel up to the yard fence and tied him.

"Shouldn't I ride him first? He hasn't had anyone on his back for almost a year," James said, as he sat down on the bed next to Randy.

"Nope. It's time for me to ride."

"OK, here we go," James said, as he picked Randy up from the bed.

James lifted and pushed until he got Randy to straddle the horse. Randy, weak as he was, managed a broad smile as he held onto the saddle horn with both hands.

"You better just lead him off first. Then when I get my balance, I can rein him myself," Randy said.

James untied Watch Joe and started leading him down the driveway. The horse walked slowly, carefully, barely picking up his feet, and setting them down carefully and deliberately so as not to jar his rider. It was as if he knew who was on him.

As James led Watch Joe, he kept looking over his shoulder at Randy. Randy was holding the saddle horn with both hands, white as a sheet. He was wobbling side-to-side from the motion of the horse—almost sliding off, but somehow managing to hold on.

"James, I can't make it," Randy said, as he began to slide from the horse.

James dropped the bridle reins and ran to Randy, catching him as he slowly slid from the saddle. James carried his unconscious brother into the house.

Randy viewed this as another setback. The infections seemed to sap all his strength. After a while this began to affect his mental attitude. Every day he became more and more despondent.

Several friends and people at Randy's church suggested he should go to Oral Roberts' Word of Faith Hospital in Tulsa, Oklahoma. The doctors there were "Spirit-filled," and if anyone could help him, they could. So Randy asked his mother to go with him to Tulsa.

Randy contacted the hospital the next day. Although he wasn't looking forward to going to another hospital, he and his mom left for Tulsa the following morning. It would take several days to run all the tests.

Upon Randy's arrival at the hospital, testing began immediately and X-rays were taken. Randy was probed, punched and examined for what seemed like an eternity. Betty stayed with him as she had done so many months before. It brought back memories of the endless hours she had spent waiting and worrying after the accident. But if there were any chance at all for recovery, she thought, it would all be worthwhile.

Randy sat in the doctor's office with Betty, waiting for the doctor to tell them about the test results. This would be his last attempt to be totally healed. Whatever the doctor told him now, he would accept as the final diagnosis.

The white-clad doctor walked in, shut the door behind him and pulled a chair up next to Randy and his mother.

"Let's have a short prayer," he said, looking at Randy and Betty. "Then we'll talk."

After prayer, the doctor leaned forward and held Randy's hand.

"Randy, short of a miracle from God, you will not walk again."

Randy swallowed hard. It was really no less than he had expected down deep inside. But now it seemed so final.

"After reviewing your tests, we feel the continuing infections and your general unhealthy condition are due mostly to your teeth. You have several teeth that are broken and abscessed. Our recommendation is that you go to a dentist and get your teeth fixed as soon as possible."

Randy was quiet on the drive back home. Once again he was feeling the pain and hopelessness of not being able to walk. But at the same time, he was encouraged. Maybe getting his teeth fixed would stop the infections. Just being able to feel better would be wonderful. Then maybe his mental attitude would improve, also. He prayed silently.

As soon as he got home, he made an appointment with Dr. Leach at Royse City. It took six months of visits twice a week to complete the dental work, but he soon began to feel better. Having his teeth fixed was an ordeal in itself. After several root canals, caps, fillings, and extractions, he was worn down and dreaded the visits. But the infections stopped and he began to gain weight. He felt he was making progress.

As his health improved, so did his mental attitude. He turned his attention from dwelling on sickness to thinking of other things. He wanted to ride a horse as he had before, and he wanted to somehow return to rodeo. To ride, he would need a special saddle; it was evident that there was no way he could ride in a standard one. So he began thinking about how to build a saddle that would give him the support he needed.

His first idea was to modify a standard saddle in such a way that he could balance. Without leg strength, that would not be easy. To begin with, he would have to be strapped in some way.

With the help of James and a neighbor, Vince Romo, Randy added what looked like the back of a stadium chair to his old saddle. The three attached the frame to the back of the cantle by screwing it into the saddle. It was a crude-looking thing, sticking up high like the back of a straight chair. But it was a start. Randy couldn't wait to try it out.

James saddled Watch Joe with the modified high-backed saddle, while Randy watched from his wheelchair.

"Man, that's a crude-looking mess," Randy commented.

"Yeah, it's crude, but it's a beginning," James answered.

James lifted Randy into the saddle, then strapped him in by running a nylon belt, like a car seat belt, around the back of the saddle and Randy's waist.

"How does it feel?" James asked.

"Better than I thought it might. At least I don't feel as if I'm going to slide off, like I did with the regular saddle."

James led Watch Joe down the driveway, glancing back at Randy to make sure this wasn't a repeat of the first day he had tried to ride. Randy held on. After a few minutes, he seemed to gain new confidence.

"Let me have the reins. And open the arena gate," Randy said.

"You sure? Should I saddle another horse and ride with you?"

"No."

James handed the reins to Randy and opened the arena gate. Randy held the reins with one hand and the saddle horn with the other.

"I'm going to walk him around the arena first to get a better feel, then kick him off into a trot. That should be the real test," Randy said, as he started off by himself.

All of his family was standing at the fence watching, almost afraid to breathe.

"What does he think he's doing?" Becky asked.

"Riding his horse," James answered, never taking his eyes off his brother.

"I think you all are crazy," Becky said, as she walked toward the house.

"Is Daddy all right?" Brett asked.

"Sure," James replied. "He's been waiting for this for a long time."

Randy continued to walk Watch Joe around the arena. He hadn't felt this carefree and alive since the accident. The more he rode, the more his confidence returned. The motion of the horse walking moved him back and forth in the saddle, and he could feel the muscles in his lower chest tightening.

He tried to cue Watch Joe to move into a trot, but all he could do was just lean forward a little. In the past, he had cued him by tightening his legs and leaning forward, but now he couldn't do either.

"I can't cue him," Randy said, riding up to the fence where James and Brett stood.

"Try giving him slack in the reins and cluck to him. Maybe that will be enough," James offered.

Randy turned and started off. He leaned forward as much as the strap and his body would allow, while moving his tongue to produce a clucking sound. Watch Joe moved into a slow trot.

Since Randy couldn't stand in the stirrups for balance to absorb the impact of the rough gait, he just bounced. The faster he went, the more he bounced, until he pulled Watch Joe up. He rode over to the fence.

"The angle is all wrong on the saddle back we added. And I've got to have some kind of padding in the saddle seat to absorb my dead weight—something that will form to me and hold me straight. And the belt has to be wider. I don't feel secure. It feels like I'm still wobbling from side to side. My legs are flying around. Somehow we need to secure my feet in the stirrups and tie them underneath the horse's stomach," Randy commented, looking down at his legs.

They spent the next several days welding another back onto the saddle. Randy used blocks of foam rubber to pad the steel rod and it seemed to be somewhat more comfortable. Not only that, but the extra padding would probably prevent a recurrence of pressure sores.

After a while, Randy started getting bored with just riding around the place, so he suggested to James that they ride over to visit their mother. Since Pa and Nanny lived next door to Betty, Randy and James would be able to show the saddle to all of them. (Their mother, Betty, and her husband, Bill, had recently moved back from Oklahoma City.) Neither of them had seen the modified saddle, or, for that matter, even knew Randy was riding a horse.

"Did you tell Mama we were riding over to see them?" James asked as he saddled Watch Joe.

"Naw, thought we'd surprise them."

"You'll surprise them all right. It might give Mama a heart attack. She doesn't even know you're riding a horse."

"Pa knows about it. He probably told Mama," Randy rationalized.

"Bet he didn't."

It was about six miles to Betty's house, mostly down back dirt roads. Vince Romo, who had helped modify the saddle, rode with them. When they rode up in front of the house, they shouted at their mother to come out.

Betty was startled when she heard all of the commotion in her front yard. She rushed to the front door, saw it was Randy on a horse, and stopped in her tracks! Her heart almost did stop.

"My God, Randy, what are you doing?"

"Riding a horse," Randy replied, smiling.

"James, why did you let him do this?" she asked, glaring at her eldest son. "I thought both of you had more sense than to pull a stunt like this. I didn't spend night and day in a hospital not knowing whether you were going to live or die to have you get hurt again," she continued.

"Mama... Mama... I'm fine," Randy interrupted. James thought the best thing for him to do was just stay out of it, so he kept quiet.

Vince stood back, trying to stay as quiet as possible.

Pa heard all the noise and came walking across the yard.

"How's it going?" Pa asked, as he walked up to Randy, smiling.

"Did you know about this?" Betty asked, looking at Pa.

"Now, Betty, you knew he wasn't going to be content sitting in a wheelchair when he could ride a horse," Pa said, putting his arm around his daughter, while winking at Randy.

"Oh, I don't know about any of you. Now let me tell you something, young man. If you get hurt on that horse, don't call me. I don't want to know about it," Betty said, pointing her finger at Randy.

"Yes, ma'am," Randy replied, smiling down at his mother. "This is Watch Joe, Mama. He'll take care of me just like I took care of him."

"You heard me... Now, do y'all want something to eat before you start home?"

"No, ma'am, we thought we'd ride on up to Royse City before we headed back," Randy teased.

"Well, just remember what I said," Betty said, going back into the house.

"Boy, did you surprise her," James whispered.

Pa laughed and walked beside his two grandsons and Vince until they crossed the road. Then he watched and waved until they disappeared around a bend in the road.

"He'll make it fine. They thought he wouldn't live through the night. Wish those doctors could see him now," Pa thought, smiling, as he walked back to his house.

After successfully modifying the standard saddle, Randy began thinking about how to design and build a new saddle, one that would provide both support and comfort. The next few days, it was all he could think about. Then one night it came to him. He knew exactly how he wanted it! He had to build it from the tree up. In the saddle seat, he could use the gel that hospitals use in bed pads to help prevent pressure sores. He could make the gel thick enough that it would form to his bony rear, act as a shock absorber, and help keep him from wobbling. It would also keep him from getting pressure sores. All it would take was time and money. They could use a big rubber band, like the barrel racers use, to hold his feet in the stirrups. And they could tie the two stirrups under Watch Joe's stomach with a strap. He couldn't wait to tell James about it.

Randy started searching for a saddletree manufacturer to build his special tree. Nothing like this had ever been built before, so he had no idea where to begin. Then he thought of a company in Welch, Oklahoma. He contacted them and became acquainted with Randy Baties. Baties agreed to work with Randy to design a special saddletree. They talked several times about how the saddletree could be built and finally decided on hardwood, reinforced with rawhide and fiberglass. The only thing Randy didn't like was that it would take Baties several months to build it. Randy sent sketches... and waited. Waiting was the hardest part of all since he had already been waiting for almost a year.

But Randy put the waiting time to good use, making plans for the future. He knew he didn't want to be tied to a tedious job as so many disabled persons are, often because of an employer's stereotypical ideas, and with no basis in an individual's ability or potential.

If he could perfect his saddle, it would give other disabled people a way to feel good about themselves. At the same time, it would provide therapy as well. The motion of a horse strengthens a person's muscles, improves coordination and builds self-confidence. When a person rides a horse, his pelvis is being moved as if he were walking. This rotation increases the strength of the trunk muscles from the shoulders to the pelvis. It also strengthens the abdominal and back muscles, even if the person is in a wheelchair.

While many horse-riding programs for the disabled have been organized all over the world, conventional saddles are usually used in these programs. Because of this, someone has to walk beside a physically disabled person, holding them on. The rider never has the opportunity to ride by himself. Randy's saddle would eliminate the need for someone to walk beside the horse holding on to the person.

While Randy continued to develop his ideas, James was still working offshore and was gone for two weeks out of the month. The rest of the time, he helped around the ranch and he and Randy rode horses. Randy rode Watch Joe and James rode Ten. James would push Randy to the saddled horses in the barn and lift him up onto Watch Joe.

Randy was still riding on the saddle with the stadium chair attached. He worked hard daily lifting weights and was now bench-pressing 125 pounds. That was a long way from the weight he had pressed before the accident, but it was also a long way from the twenty-five pounds he had managed the first time he attempted to lift at Baylor. His weight was up from one hundred pounds to 120 pounds, and he thought now for the first time that he was really recovering.

After Thanksgiving it turned cold and the rain started. Once more Randy found himself confined inside, and it was pure torture. He became like a caged animal, arguing with everyone and being demanding. He called about the saddletree two or three times a week.

Cold weather had never before bothered Randy, but that winter he found himself getting colder and colder. He would turn the heater up until everyone else was sweating, then they would turn it down. It became a constant battle. It was evident they all were experiencing "cabin fever," and they looked forward to spring.

Christmas was only a couple of weeks away when Randy decided he wanted to do his own Christmas shopping.

Becky had offered to shop for him, if he would tell her what he wanted her to buy. But Randy wanted to do it himself. It was time he got out in public, he said.

So James and Randy drove to a shopping mall. As they pulled into the parking lot, Randy began having second thoughts. Maybe this wasn't as good an idea as he had thought. There were cars going in every direction and people hurrying about. It looked scary from the safety of the car.

"Sure you want to do this?" James asked, as he set up Randy's wheelchair.

"No, I'm not... but we're here. Might as well give it a try," Randy replied, lifting himself into the wheelchair.

As James pushed him toward the door, Randy couldn't help watching every car they passed behind. He expected every one of them to back out over him. For the first time he realized that he was lower than everything else. He had to look up at everything and everybody, and it frightened him.

When they got into the shopping mall, it wasn't any better. People were hurrying about and several people ran into him. One lady even fell over him. Most acted as if he had no business being there, and if they offered an apology, it was brief and usually gruff.

Getting on the elevator was another experience. People packed in around him. Again, he felt as if they were all going to step on him. As he looked around, all he could see were legs and feet. It was devastating. He felt as if he needed to wheel away from there as fast as he could. If he could have walked, he would have broken and run as soon as the elevator opened. Indeed, by the time the elevator door opened, his mouth was dry and his head pounded.

Randy sits between his grandparents, Nanny and Pa, in 1960. Pa played a vital role in Randy's life, particularly after the accident. *Credit: Bird Collection*

With his fishing pole in hand, Randy stands with his great-granddaddy, "Big Jim" Barefield. Randy's family ties were to mean a lot to him. *Credit: Bird Collection*

At age 12, Randy with Red and Dusty, the prizes he reaped from the family reunion Pa had organized at Trinity Valley Ranch. *Credit: Bird Collection*

Randy with his arm around Sugarfoot, the colt from Belle, the horse James had picked that memorable day at Trinity Valley Ranch. *Credit: Bird Collection*

Family portrait, 1970. Randy, Peggy, and James pose with their parents, Jim and Betty. *Credit: Bird Collection*

Randy returns the punt for a touchdown in his high-school game in 1972. *Credit: Bird Collection*

In 1971, Randy was also on the Tomball High School track team. Here he is with Joe Featherston (left), and Jim and Joe Warren, who are standing on either side of Randy. *Credit: Bird Collection*

A year after graduating from Tomball High School in 1973, Randy married Donna. *Credit: Bird Collection*

Feeling indestructible, Randy rides a bucking horse in January 1986, a month before the accident that would change his life. *Credit: Bird Collection*

Brett was born in 1975, and is seen here at age 1, practicing riding his toy horse.
Credit: Bird Collection

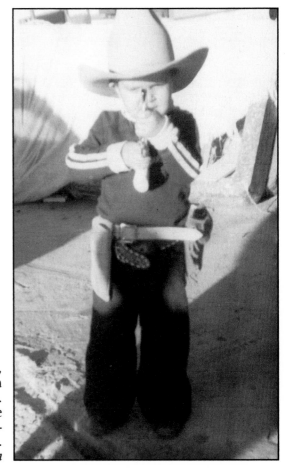

Still a young cowboy in training, Brett shoots the camera at age 3, a year before his parents divorced. Brett would reach his teens before he really began to love the cowboy life his father exemplifies.
Credit: Bird Collection

James and Randy, on either side of their mother, Betty, with their grandmother, Nanny, on the right. Randy's family was a continuing source of strength and encouragement in the difficult years after his accident. *Credit: Bird Collection*

In 1987, after much soul-searching, Donna generously agreed to let Brett live with his father. Brett played football for Caddo Mills Middle School. *Credit: Bird Collection*

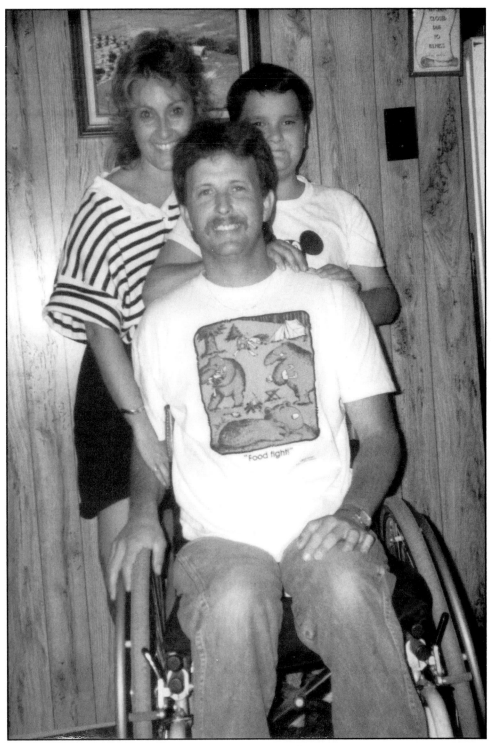

Donna, Randy, and Brett seen together in May 1988, after Brett was living with Randy full time. Brett's new active lifestyle would transform him into a lean, fit teenager. *Credit: Bird Collection*

Randy was determined to find a way to ride competitively again. In his first competition after the accident, at Greenville, Texas, he used his prototype saddle—and won! *Credit: Bird Collection*

The rodeo clowns play a vital role in saving cowboys from serious injury by distracting the bull after a cowboy has been thrown. *Credit: Bird Collection*

James heads a cow while Randy, with rope in hand, heels it. The brothers had always been great friends, and the accident seemed to solidify the relationship even more. James and Randy trained and rode together in competition for some time before James retired from the rodeo circuit. *Credit: Greenville Banner*

Randy acknowledges the crowd's applause after a Super Bull Tour performance in Abilene, Texas. Randy's performance is often greeted with a standing ovation.
Credit: Doyle Keeton, Sports Unlimited

James and Randy check the belly band on Randy's saddle. The wide band attached to the saddle back gives Randy stability, helps him balance, and allows him to lean forward while he's roping.
Credit: Bird Collection

Wherever Randy goes on the Super Bull Tour, people are amazed at his story. Local media frequently run stories about his remarkable return to professional rodeo. Here, Randy autographs copies of a local newspaper after a 1991-92 Super Bull performance. Brett is standing beside his father. *Credit: Doyle Keeton, Sports Unlimited*

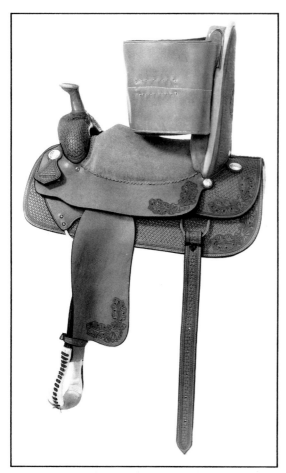

After much trial and error and many modifications, the saddle Randy hopes will restore dignity and a measure of control to the disabled—the Randy Bird Therapy Saddle—is now available. *Credit: Bird Collection*

Randy puts the first layer of leather on one of his saddles, which he now sells to disabled people as far away as Australia. *Credit: Ron Westmoreland*

In 1982, Randy bought this 90-year-old house, which he later enclosed in his new house. *Credit: Bird Collection*

Randy wheels himself up the ramp to his home. The one-room cabin shown above has been transformed into this lovely ranch house. *Credit: Ron Westmoreland*

At home in Texas, Randy practices roping a steer. *Credit: Bryan Westmoreland*

Brett and Randy riding. The father-and-son duo share an unusually close relationship. *Credit: Ron Westmoreland*

Uncharacteristically without a hat, Randy lets his rope fly to lasso the heels of a steer. *Credit: Ron Westmoreland*

Randy eyes a steer before he starts to lasso it. *Credit: Ron Westmoreland*

Randy in action, roping a steer. "There's nothing I can't do. I just have to find a different way to do it," Randy says. *Credit: Bryan Westmoreland*

In 1990, Randy married a young widow with two children. Here, Randy, Brett, Matthew, Christina, and Marilyn are pictured on their front porch near Quinlan, Texas. *Credit: Ron Westmoreland*

"Get me off here, quick," Randy shouted.

James rapidly pushed him away from the elevator and the crowd of people rushing out.

"Man... I couldn't take much more of that," Randy said, wiping the sweat from his forehead.

"What's wrong?" James asked.

"I just realized that everyone is taller than I am. I can't see over the crowd. Everything is just closed around me. All I can see are people's legs and feet, and they all look like they're going to either run over me or step on me. Man, it's scary!"

After several hours of being pushed, shoved, and stepped on, Randy managed to get his shopping done. And even though the whole process was physically and mentally painful, he felt as if he had accomplished something. He had survived Christmas shopping. He figured that if he could survive that mob of people at their worst, maybe he could make it under normal conditions.

After Christmas, Randy decided it was time to make good on his promise to visit the Baylor Rehabilitation Center. He called before he went to make sure it would be all right. The staff was very supportive of his plan to visit.

He told Becky and James he wanted to go by himself. He wanted the people to see first-hand that a paralyzed person could make it on his own.

The morning he was to go, he spent an unusual amount of time dressing. He wanted to look extra good. He wanted people to know that you didn't have to look and act differently just because you had a disability. Too many disabled persons acted and looked disabled, Randy thought.

He vowed he would never look or act as if he were paralyzed.

It was a cold and dreary February morning when Randy finally pulled into the parking lot at Baylor Rehabilitation Center. As he parked and turned the engine off, he glanced at the hospital. All the way there he had been telling himself that it was just a visit, and there was no need to be nervous. He wanted to be calm and confident.

He opened the truck door, and, after retrieving his wheelchair from behind the seat, set it down on the pavement beside the open door. By grasping the truck door with his left hand and holding on to the steering wheel with his right hand, he lowered himself into the wheelchair. He then rolled himself back, closing and locking the door.

His thoughts went back to that day in May when he had gone through this door on his way out of the hospital. It brought back memories he had thought were forgotten. Once he even stopped. Everything in him was telling him to turn around and go home. But he swallowed hard, and continued up the winding sidewalk.

Once inside the elevator, he pushed the second floor button. A cold chill went up his back. It brought back the memory of that first day, when the elevator doors had opened and he had thought that it was just another hospital. Later he had realized he was wrong—it was more, much more than that. Finally, Randy had come to understand that, even though the people helping him couldn't totally relate to his feelings of frustration and the fear that gripped him, they could and would help.

That had to be part of the message he wanted to share. He also wanted to give the patients hope and let them know their life was not over! They just might have to make it a different way. There are always alternatives and adjustments. They just had to explore them and deal with them.

Randy received a warm welcome from the staff, even those he hadn't considered very friendly when he was there. But when he saw Nancy, the emotion he had managed to repress erupted. She stood in a doorway with her arms crossed, smiling as the throng of well-wishers gathered around Randy. He smiled, excused himself, and slowly wheeled toward Nancy. She waited for him to come to a complete stop in front of her, then she reached down and hugged him.

"Hello, Randy Bird. It's been a while."

Randy couldn't speak. He wrapped his arms around her, holding her close. It had been a long time, too long.

"So how are you?" Nancy asked, straightening up.

"Better," Randy replied, wiping tears from his eyes. "I kept telling myself this wasn't going to happen, but it all came flooding back."

"It's part of the healing, so don't fight it. Save your strength for the real battles."

They talked about what Randy had been doing since he had been released, and Nancy told him about various patients, past and present.

He spent the entire day going from room to room, visiting each patient. He would talk and answer questions if they wanted, or sit quietly if they didn't or couldn't talk. He spoke with them about their fears and about the future. He offered encouragement, and would pray with them if that was what they wanted. But most of all, he stressed that there is always hope, and that with God's help and their own personal determination they could make it.

By the time he headed out of the parking lot, Randy was mentally and physically drained. But he had a warm, satisfied feeling because he knew he could and would make a difference.

Randy began to watch the calendar. On February 23, he felt an eerie dread all day. He thought about the accident and how his life had changed drastically since then. He tried desperately not to dwell on the negative things, but the horrifying events of the past crept into his consciousness.

That night he relived the entire accident. He woke himself up shouting, and began to shake uncontrollably.

"What was that?" James asked, as he became aware of Randy shouting.

"I didn't hear anything," Becky said, sitting up.

"It's Randy," James said alarmed.

James threw the covers back and hurried to Randy's bedroom.

"What's wrong, Bubba?" James asked, as he squatted next to Randy's bed.

"Nightmares," Randy replied, in a weak, shaky voice.

"Having the shakes again?" James asked, as he pulled the covers back and lay next to Randy.

Randy never answered as James put his arms around his brother.

"Will it ever stop?" Randy whispered.

"Sure it will."

James held his brother until the shaking stopped and Randy finally went to sleep.

Chapter 10

Spring eventually rolled around, and with it came the promise of warm, sun-filled days. It was a time for new beginnings. Trees were leafing out, grass was turning green, and the horses were shedding their long, winter hair. Randy felt as if it were a new beginning for him as well.

Pa visited often, as did Randy's mother and father. But aware of his desire to take care of himself, they limited their help and tried not to show their concern.

James was still working offshore every two weeks, returning as soon as his shift ended. He told Randy he was thinking about quitting and getting a job in the Dallas area. He couldn't see why he should return to the coast when the rest of the family lived here.

Becky continued to run the household. She watched over Randy like a mother hen. The children seemed to get along well together and sometimes the ranch house vibrated from the youthful energy of James' and Becky's children, Amy and Cody, and Randy's son, Brett.

When the long-awaited saddletree was delivered, Randy felt like a child at Christmas. It was just a rugged piece of hardwood covered with rawhide and fiberglass, but to

Randy it was beautiful. It was more than just a saddletree: it was freedom, and one of the first steps toward regaining his old life as a rodeo cowboy.

Randy had contacted Juan Vega, a local saddle maker, to build the saddle to Randy's specifications. So when the tree arrived, Randy and Brett hurried to Juan's shop.

Juan thought it was the strangest thing he had ever seen, but said he would try his best to complete the saddle. It would take a couple of months, he said, a time that seemed endless to Randy.

Everything that had happened since the accident had taken longer than he expected. And patience had never been one of Randy's virtues.

The saddle was finally ready. Randy had made several trips to the saddle shop just to watch the progress and to make sure it was being built the way he wanted. This saddle would be a first. To his knowledge, it was the only saddle ever built strictly for the purpose of providing support for a disabled person. Randy had also designed it to be strong enough for roping, a fact that no one except James knew about. While it was obvious Randy couldn't ride rough stock again, he hoped he could compete in team roping as a heeler. He had two goals for the saddle: to help other disabled riders, and to help himself rodeo again.

He couldn't wait to get home and try out the saddle.

But James wouldn't be back until later that day, so Randy would have to wait a little longer. More waiting! One thing the therapist and instructors at Baylor had kept telling him was certainly true: he would always have to depend on others for some things. But he tried constantly to eliminate as much dependence on others as possible.

Randy was waiting on the front porch when James pulled into the long gravel driveway leading to the house. By the time James crossed the cattle guard, Randy was wheeling down the ramp. He motioned to James to follow him to the barn.

James couldn't imagine what Randy wanted. He thought something had happened to one of the horses. He stopped his car and jumped out, running to catch up with Randy.

"Look," Randy pointed at the saddle. "Isn't it something?"

"My God, Randy, I thought something was wrong," James said, relieved.

"Man, let's get this on my horse," Randy said, ignoring James' remark. "I've been waiting since this morning."

"I worked last night and just drove for six hours, and you want me to saddle a horse before I even see my wife and kids?" James asked, staring at his brother.

"Everybody is fine. Let's get Watch Joe saddled."

"Great... can't even get in the house," James muttered, as he grabbed a halter from the tack room.

James picked up the squeaky saddle and placed it on Watch Joe's back. The horse didn't like the new smell and feel of the saddle, so he stiffened and turned his head to look it over.

"Looks kind of different, don't it?" James commented, as he tightened up the cinch.

"That cantle does stick up high," Randy said, eyes fixed on the saddle. "But ain't it purty?"

"It sure ought to do the job. You ready to try it out?"

"Man, am I ready!" Randy said, moving his wheelchair closer.

James reached down, cupping his arms under Randy's legs. Then, as Randy put his arms around James' neck, James lifted him up. Standing next to the horse, James could lift Randy up to where he could grab the saddle horn and help pull himself up to straddle the saddle.

"I can tell you're gaining weight," James said, catching his breath. James and Randy had been about the same size before the accident.

"Hey, man, this is great!" Randy said, pulling himself straight in the saddle. "Adjust the stirrups as best as you can... I'm ready to try it out."

James adjusted the length of the stirrups. The new leather was stiff and hard to twist.

"This wide belt is going to be great," Randy commented, as he pulled the nylon belt tight around his stomach and lower chest.

James removed the rubber bands from the old modified saddle and secured Randy's feet in the stirrups.

"You want me to lead him around first?" James asked, looking up at Randy.

"Just hand me the reins and look out," Randy replied, pushing his black hat snug down on his head.

James had barely opened the arena gate before Randy and Watch Joe shot through the opening.

Randy trotted around the arena until he felt secure, then he popped Watch Joe with the reins to urge him to move smoothly into a short lope.

Randy couldn't hold back his enthusiasm any longer.

"This is it! Man, we've done it!" he shouted.

After several turns around the arena, he pulled back on the reins and Watch Joe slid to a stop. Randy rode up to where James stood smiling. Becky and the children had heard the shouting and had come out to watch.

"Hey, I've got to get cleaned up and get some rest before I go to sleep on my feet," James said, yawning.

"Go ahead," Randy said, "I'll be right here when you get through."

"It might take me a while."

"I'm OK. If I need something, Brett can help me."

Randy rode around and around the arena for hours. Everyone else went back into the house, but Randy had waited too long for this day. He wasn't about to stop.

After the initial delight of riding again subsided, he began to seriously evaluate the saddle. One thing that was immediately noticeable was the position of the saddle back. It leaned too far back, so that it was difficult for Randy to see directly in front of the horse. That would make it harder to rope a steer's back legs, because he wouldn't be able to see them until the steer was almost out of roping position.

It was mid-afternoon before James came outside and walked up to the fence.

"Hey, you going to stay out here all night?" James shouted.

"Can't. Don't have any lights," Randy answered smiling.

"Well, what do you think?" James asked, as Randy rode up to the fence.

"The back of the saddle leans too far back. Since I can't lean forward, it throws me back looking at the sky instead of where I'm going. It'll be kind of tough to rope a steer from that position."

Anatomy of a Therapy Saddle

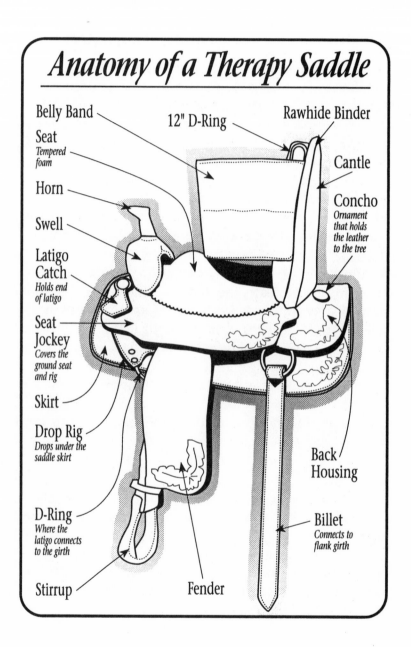

Belly Band

Seat
Tempered foam

Horn

Swell

Latigo Catch
Holds end of latigo

Seat Jockey
Covers the ground seat and rig

Skirt

Drop Rig
Drops under the saddle skirt

D-Ring
Where the latigo connects to the girth

Stirrup

12" D-Ring

Rawhide Binder

Cantle

Concho
Ornament that holds the leather to the tree

Back Housing

Billet
Connects to flank girth

Fender

Anatomy of a Western Saddle

Horn

Swell

Latigo
Catch

Seat
Jockey

Skirt

D-Ring

Stirrup

Seat

Cantle

Concho

Back
Housing

Billet

Fender

"Yeah, but how's everything else?"

"Well... I feel secure and I'm not wobbling, but the nylon band could be just a little wider," Randy said, slapping the wide band around his waist. "Boy, my upper chest muscles are already getting sore."

"You about ready to call it a day? You're looking a little tired," James said.

"Yeah, guess I'd better. But man, this has been a great day!" Randy smiled.

James followed Randy to the barn and lifted him from the horse into his wheelchair.

"Sure feel low down after riding so long," Randy commented.

"I bet you do," James said, as he unsaddled the horse.

"We're going to get there. For the first time I really believe I'm going to make it back," Randy said, as he positioned himself next to Watch Joe and reached out to pet him on the shoulder. "We're going to rodeo yet."

Whenever the unpredictable spring weather permitted, and when James was there to help him, Randy rode his new saddle, taking note of everything he thought would make it better or easier to produce. It was difficult for him to sleep at night, since the saddle was so constantly on his mind.

One morning as Randy and James were eating breakfast, Randy talked for the first time about producing the saddle commercially.

"I'm thinking about mass-producing the saddle," Randy said, looking at James' reaction.

"How and where? It'll take money to get started."

"I don't have all the answers, but after this next saddle, I'll have a usable design."

"Yeah, but who will be able to afford it? That first one cost a small fortune," James added, trying not to sound negative, but being realistic.

"It would have to be priced where people could afford it, but it would never be competitive with standard saddles, because it's not a standard saddle. The tree is at least twice the cost of the standard tree. Any time you produce something special, it's going to cost more. But look what this saddle can do for physically challenged people all over the world. There just has to be a market for it," Randy said.

"I agree totally, and I'm with you all the way," James replied.

For the next several weeks, Randy's thoughts were directed towards producing the saddle. He talked with several saddle makers in the area, but none of them seemed interested. The negative response dampened his enthusiasm a little, but he wasn't about to give up on the idea. He had to keep on thinking and explore every opportunity.

Pa and Randy decided it would be a good time to sell their cows and calves. The cattle market was up, pastures were in good shape, and Randy could use the money.

Randy enlisted the help of two of his rodeo friends, Jay Sorrels and Stanley Giles, and a neighbor, Kevin Laffavor, just in case the cows didn't want to be cooperative.

Randy also planned on using his two stock dogs, Rooster and Hock. Rooster would be a lot of help in pushing the cattle out of the brush, and Hock would keep the cattle going after they were in the open. The only problem with Hock was that she didn't always keep the cattle going in the right direction.

Hock had gotten her name because she would run behind a slow-moving cow and bite at its hocks to get it going. However, she didn't care if the stock were traveling in the right direction or not. In fact, she had a habit of running cattle away from the pen.

Randy, James, and Pa hooked up Randy's trailer and started down the dirt road to the cow pasture. Jay, Stanley, and Kevin followed with another truck and trailer.

Randy was pulling an empty trailer. He was going to transport some cattle to the auction barn while the others were being rounded up.

He shouted at Rooster and Hock to get in the back of the truck. The stock dogs eagerly leapt into the truck bed, running from side to side in anticipation.

After arriving at the pasture, Randy backed the long stock trailer up to the cattle-pen loading ramp. James, Stanley, Jay, Kevin, and Pa gathered around the truck cab.

"What I thought we'd do is put out a little feed in the pen, and sucker what cows we could to come in. We'll close them in and load 'em up. Then I'll take that bunch on over to the sale barn. We probably ought to handle the bull by himself. The ones we can't trap, we'll just have to get the best way we can. Jay, you and Stanley might have to rope a couple of the bad-acting cows... but I think that most of them will come to feed," Randy said.

"We can use Rooster and Hock to move 'em along," James added.

"Yeah, if Hock don't run 'em the wrong way," Randy

said, smiling.

They were able to get all the cattle loaded, with the exception of the bull and three cows. After a lot of wild chases down gullies and through brush that ripped clothes and skin alike, all the cows and calves were penned.

As they were loading the bull, Hock was biting at its back legs, making it harder to load it. Randy shouted at Hock to stop, so she ran under the truck and laid down. After they got the bull loaded, Randy started to move the truck. As he did, he heard James shout.

"You ran over Hock!"

Randy's heart was beating rapidly as he opened the door and looked toward the back of the truck. James picked up Hock and carried her to the truck cab.

"Man, she's limp as a rag. She's dead, Randy."

"No, she's not. Put her in the truck. I'm taking her to the vet."

Blood was beginning to seep from Hock's closed mouth and she didn't seem to be breathing.

James laid her on the seat next to Randy as Randy started the truck.

"I'll be back as soon as I can," Randy said, as he put the truck into motion.

Randy kept looking over at the motionless dog and thinking that she was dead. He had to try to save her. No one had thought he would live either, so he wasn't ready to give up on her. One thing he had learned from his experience was that you don't just give up. No one except God knows what is going to happen.

"Lord, don't let her die," Randy said out loud, as he turned to look at the small dog who was lying deathly still.

Before they arrived at the vet clinic, Hock jerked all over, then sat up and looked at Randy.

"Well, girl, you're not dead after all!" Randy exclaimed.

Randy left Hock at the vet's and returned to the pasture. As he drove up, James walked up to the truck with Pa.

"Sorry about Hock," James said.

"Hey, don't be sorry. She has a broken leg, but the vet says she will be fine," Randy said, smiling.

"Isn't that something? I figured she was dead for sure. The trailer wheels rolled right over her. And the bull was in the trailer. He has to weigh fifteen hundred pounds," James said.

"Yeah, how can you figure it? I remember a lot of people giving up on me... It's all really up to the Lord," Randy said, looking at Pa.

Pa smiled knowingly.

Hock's right leg had been broken and she had experienced nerve damage that would cause permanent paralysis in that leg. But she lived and was able to continue working cattle on three legs. Randy thought she seemed to run faster and be even more agile on three than she had been on four!

She never lost her zeal for life... just like her master.

Chapter 11

It was late summer. The combination of temperatures reaching one hundred degrees and a lack of rain was causing vegetation to burn up. Hay for winter was already stacked in the barn and the fields had been plowed in preparation for fall planting. Randy had modified the tractor so that he could operate it. It provided him with the flexibility to accomplish many of the day-to-day tasks around the ranch without assistance.

His face and arms were changing to a deep brown from what he had referred to as "sickly white." And his strength and vitality continued to improve. In addition, he kept discovering better ways to do many everyday tasks. His small workshop next to the barn yielded all sorts of mechanical aids.

He was now ready for the final step in his rehabilitation. He wanted to be completely on his own, but as long as James and Becky were always there to make sure he had everything, Randy would never know if he could take care of himself and Brett.

The problem was he didn't know how to approach James and Becky about it. There was no doubt that, without their help, love, and caring, he wouldn't be where he was now.

But somehow he had to move on. He thought constantly about how to tell them in a way that wouldn't hurt their feelings. But the words wouldn't come.

Randy hired two local welders to modify the arena so he would be able to rope steers. But they could work only early in the morning and late in the afternoon because of the heat. Friends and neighbors would drop by and work occasionally, but even then, the project was going too slowly for Randy. So he started doing some of the work himself.

He would wheel himself up to where he could reach whatever needed welding, then he would put on the welder's hood and begin welding. From time to time a passerby would shout at Randy, telling him that a fire had started under his wheelchair or that his pants were smoldering. Randy would beat out the fire with a glove, wave to the passerby, and return to welding.

Brett would help his father when Randy insisted, but he preferred being inside where it was cool, watching television or playing video games with his cousins. Brett had been raised in the city for the first ten years of his life, so ranch life didn't have the special appeal for him that it had for Randy.

However, it was Randy's dream that Brett would follow in his footsteps and come to love horses and ranch life the way he did. He wanted to be close to Brett and share with him all the wonders that ranch life provided. He felt discouraged when it seemed that Brett didn't share his enthusiasm. But maybe, Randy thought, it would come, in time.

By September the arena was complete. Randy leveled the

ground inside the arena, then plowed it. As he sat on the tractor looking at what had been accomplished, he removed his hat and bowed his head, thanking God for his many blessings.

One afternoon as James and Randy were sitting on the front porch talking about buying steers, Randy decided the time was right to talk about going out on his own.

"James, I've got to talk to you about something," Randy said.

"What is it?" James asked, turning his head so that he could see Randy.

"I don't want to hurt your feelings or Becky's. That's the last thing I want to do. But I've got to be on my own. I've got to find out if I can take care of myself and Brett. And I'll never do it with y'all taking care of me."

James continued to look at Randy without answering. Then he finally spoke.

"Well, if that's what you want..." he answered, looking at the porch floor.

"But I don't want y'all to have your feelings hurt. I couldn't have made it this far without y'all. It don't have anything to do with not appreciating what y'all have done or how much I love you. I just got to start doing for myself. You understand, don't you?"

"Yeah, I do. But I'm not sure Becky will," James said, as he slowly got up from the chair and walked into the house.

James, Becky, and their two children moved not far from Randy's place a few weeks later. They had been hurt, but Randy hoped that love would overcome hurt feelings in time.

134

Randy bought thirty roping steers and made plans to hold jackpot ropings on Sunday afternoons. He didn't have lights in the arena yet, so he couldn't rope in the evenings.

During the ropings, it would take several men to work the steers. Roping bonnets would have to be put on the steers' horns to keep the ropes from burning their heads, and someone would have to take the ropes off the horns as soon as the steers were roped. Then someone else would have to move them back to the chutes and open the gate.

To accomplish these tasks, Randy enlisted the help of several of Brett's friends who lived in the area. Randy agreed to pay them based on the number of ropers he had on a given day. If there were fifty teams, he would pay the boys more than if there were ten teams.

Before the first roping, Randy sat Brett down and talked to him.

"Brett, you have got to help me on this. I mean it's not something you can just shrug off. It's going to be hot, dusty work. But it's a chance for us to make some money, so we have to make it work. And it'll give us a way to have cattle to practice on. I hope you'll want to start riding and want to rope. If you do, we'll get you a horse of your own, one that you can train yourself. Would you like that?"

"I guess," Brett answered, without enthusiasm.

"Well, we'll see. But you've got to be a man now and show the other boys you can do it. OK?"

"Yes, sir."

Until the weather turned cold and the winter rains came, Randy held ropings. There was a lot of complaining and a few of Brett's friends got knocked around some by the steers.

There were even a few toes that got stepped on, but other than that, it worked fine.

Randy took Brett's video games and locked them away. There just wasn't time for television or playing games. They had work to do.

After a while, Randy and Brett became inseparable, working side by side sometimes from dawn until dusk. Brett became Randy's willing legs and constant companion. In only a few short months, he emerged from a soft, chubby boy to a lean, tanned young man. When Randy looked at his son, it was evident he liked what he saw.

Several of the boys who had helped Randy with the ropings decided they would like to ride the steers if it was all right with him. Randy told them it was OK if their parents didn't mind. If they received permission, Randy let them ride after the roping was over.

Randy was concerned when Brett wanted to ride the steers, but he didn't try to discourage him. Before his accident, Randy had thought he could do anything and never be hurt. Now he knew better, and he couldn't help but be concerned about Brett riding.

There were so many things that could happen, and he lived in fear that Brett would be hurt as he had been. He couldn't stand for him to be injured. Now he knew how his parents must have felt when he was riding broncs, and when he was injured—it has to be every parent's nightmare to have a child injured or killed.

But, despite his fears, Randy went with Brett to buy him a bull rope and all the equipment it took to ride with, hoping all the time he wouldn't want to ride.

After the roping, all the boys were excited about riding the steers. Randy asked a couple of the cowboys to help them and they tied a steer to a post. After it was let out, the cowboys would hold the steer while the bull rope was tightened. One by one, the boys would try to ride the bucking steer. The first few times no one rode and they all swallowed a lot of sand. But as they gained experience, they began to stay on longer.

One night Randy was out in the arena in his wheelchair, as was his practice when the boys were riding. Brett was going to ride one of the largest and meanest steers. The steer had been named the Schlitz Malt Liquor Bull because he looked like the bull in the television commercial.

The steer was tied to a post as were all the rest, and turned out so the cowboys could put the bull rope on. But this time Randy didn't get far enough away. The steer had more slack in the rope than Randy had thought he had. The steer ran out of the chute and headed for Randy with his horns leveled. Randy quickly began wheeling himself away but the deep sand restricted his speed.

Brett and the others saw the steer bounding toward Randy and ran to try to head it off, but the steer was too fast.

Knowing the steer was close, Randy glanced over his shoulder. As he did, the steer slammed his lowered horns into Randy's back, sending him sprawling face-first into the deep sand. The impact knocked the breath out of Randy, and his first thought was that the impact had damaged the rod in his back. Then panic set in.

He grabbed his back, expecting to feel the rod extruding through the skin. But it felt all right. He didn't feel any pain at all.

He was still spitting out sand when the cowboys rushed up to him. They lifted him up and sat him back into his wheelchair. As they all looked nervously at him, he began to laugh, much to their relief. "Man, that sucker could run! He almost got me."

"What do you mean 'almost'?" one of the concerned cowboys asked.

"You all right?" Brett asked, visibly shaken.

"Sure, I'm all right. It'll take more than a hooking from an ol' steer to get me," Randy said, turning to where he could see Brett.

Randy was smiling on the outside, but on the inside he was sick. What if the impact had disturbed the surgery? He couldn't go through another year of hospitals.

As everyone moved away and Brett prepared to ride, Randy watched Brett mount the steer. He realized he was doing the things that the therapist at Baylor had told him not to do. He was putting himself at risk. And for what?

He watched as Brett was thrown hard, got up, dusted himself off, and walked over.

"Dad, I think I would like to learn how to rope," Brett said, as he squatted down next to his father.

"Good, we'll get started tomorrow," Randy said smiling, relieved that this might be the end of Brett's bull-riding career. He didn't think he could make it through Brett's riding stock as he had done. "Being a parent gives you a different outlook," he thought.

During the next few weeks, Randy thought a lot about the risks he was taking and the life he wanted for himself and Brett. He decided that the risks were worth it. Nothing in life is for sure. You just have to follow your dreams and trust in the Lord.

Brett started riding Watch Joe, with Randy giving him advice on how to handle the horse properly. Brett learned quickly, and it wasn't long before he was cutting cattle. Randy wanted him to know how to set a cutting horse before he started roping. It would be a good, basic lesson in horsemanship.

One particular day, Brett was moving cattle around in the arena when a steer made a quick move to the right. Watch Joe darted after the animal. Then, just as quickly, the steer reversed its direction. Watch Joe dropped his head and switched ends in an attempt to block the steer. But when the horse turned sharply, Brett didn't. He landed in a heap on the sandy ground.

Randy wheeled himself to where Brett was brushing himself off.

"Are you OK?" Randy asked, concerned about his son.

"Yes, sir," Brett replied, embarrassed, but not hurt.

"Let me tell you something, Brett. It's something I've heard all my life," Randy said, helping Brett dust himself off. "The only people that never fall off a horse or never get bucked off just don't ride a horse. Anyone, I don't care how good a rider they are, is going to hit the dirt," he said, patting Brett on the back. "Now catch ol' Watch Joe and try it again."

Brett worked hard at learning how to ride and, by the end of the summer, had begun to make progress.

One evening after the animals were fed and cared for and Brett and Randy were finishing supper, Randy looked over at his son. He thought about how hard all this had been on him. He and Donna had divorced when Brett was four. Then had come the accident and the long months of illness that followed, then the paralysis. But through it all, Brett had adapted.

"Son, I'm proud of you," Randy said, smiling.

"Thanks, Dad," Brett replied, returning his father's smile.

"Hasn't been easy sometimes, has it?" Randy continued.

"No, sir."

"But we're going to make it. Right?"

"Yes, sir."

"Well, tomorrow's another day. Guess we'd better get this mess cleaned up. You've got school in the morning and that school bus won't wait," Randy said, as he backed away from the table with a load of dishes in his lap.

"No, sir, they sure won't wait," Brett said, as he began picking up dishes. "Dad, do you think we could go to Nanny and Pa's house for supper this weekend? I'm sure getting tired of frozen dinners."

"Sure," Randy smiled, "But I'll start cooking again. It just seems like we don't have time for cooking or cleaning any more."

Randy made a special prayer of thanks that night.

Randy built a roping dummy out of steel pipes and rods. It had the appearance of a real steer, even to the head and horns. He would sit on Watch Joe and throw loop after loop at the back legs. Then he would have another horse-mounted cowboy pull the dummy steer along while he rode up behind and threw at the back legs as if he were heeling a real steer. It helped him begin to perfect his heel loop and build up his right arm.

In the beginning his arm would tire after a few throws. As he gained strength, he would rope for hours—throwing, recoiling the rope, and throwing again. Practice was the only way he could perfect the loop.

After several weeks, Randy moved from the roping dummy to trailing along behind another mounted cowboy and roping at his horse's back legs. Most horses didn't mind, but every once in a while one would object and kick at the rope.

Several of the cowboys who came to the ropings helped install lights around the arena. Having lights would let Randy hold ropings at night.

When they were installing the lights, Randy seemed to be everywhere. One minute he would be behind the chutes, straining to wheel himself through the deep sand. Then he would be in his truck, driving slowly around the catch pen as the electrical cable was being strung from light pole to light pole. These were cowboys helping cowboys. None accepted pay for their many hours of labor.

Randy was able to hold only a few ropings before the rain and cold weather brought it all to a halt. Winter was hard on Randy, with the inclement weather restricting his outside activities. But the horses and steers still had to be fed and cared for, even when it rained and the cold north wind blew.

As Randy gained strength and weight, he seemed to be able to withstand the cold weather better, but he still suffered. Without movement in his legs, his body would become chilled to the bone as the cold crept up his body. Because he had no feeling in his lower torso, he had to be constantly aware of the dangers of frostbite and hypothermia. Sometimes he would have Brett feel him to make sure he wasn't getting dangerously cold.

Even though the Texas winters were not very long, they gave Randy an opportunity to reflect on what had happened in the previous months and to plan for the future.

He was very seldom sick any more and was gaining strength every month. He still had a long way to go to get his upper-body strength back to where it was before the accident, but he was making progress.

Brett was becoming more and more help to him and was growing into a responsible young man. Randy would laugh out loud at some of the predicaments they both managed to get into.

He remembered the first time he had tried to get on and off the tractor with Brett helping him. They finally managed to get him into the tractor seat with lots of pulling and pushing. But when he attempted to get down, it was a different story.

Randy was easing himself down from the tractor seat with Brett under him, pushing and pulling. But Randy's grasp on the steering wheel slipped and he fell on top of Brett. Both landed in a heap underneath the tractor. After Brett saw that his father wasn't hurt, he and Randy had a good laugh.

Randy had learned over the past year that he was tougher than he had thought. He had found out that he wouldn't break in two when he pushed himself, as he had been led to believe would happen. The episode of the steer running him over was a perfect example.

Without realizing it, Randy and Brett were forging a bond that would never be broken. It went further than a normal father-and-son relationship. Randy relied on Brett almost as much as Brett relied on his father. It was, and is still, a special relationship.

Randy was still concerned about the future. He wanted to return to the cowboy lifestyle, but he realized he had to make a living for himself and Brett. What he wanted to do with the rest of his life seemed simple to him. He wanted to be in a position where he and Brett were financially secure, and he wanted to help other people with physical handicaps overcome their disabilities.

One way he could help was to make his saddle available to the disabled. And he planned on visiting as many rehabilitation centers as would invite him. Also, he wanted to participate in rodeo again. It seemed his best opportunity would be in team roping.

He wanted to give back some of what had been given him. He wanted to give hope to people that didn't have any. His message would be that it's never too late. There's a way, no matter what the odds. All it takes is faith, determination, desire, dedication, and God's healing hands.

Chapter 12

In mid-spring of 1988, Randy started holding team ropings at his arena. Winter had been slow to give way to the warmer, dryer weather of early spring. And when it came, it was only for a short while. Then the late spring rains came with a vengeance. The arena stood in a foot of water at times and the runoff gouged two-foot deep crevasses in the sand.

It was discouraging for Randy and Brett to watch through the window as the rain pelted down, washing away what they worked so hard to build. And, through all the rain and flooding, they still had to feed the horses and steers.

Randy hadn't talked with James much since they moved and he missed their long conversations and his company. But maybe when the rains stopped and the weather cleared they could begin roping together. It was still Randy's dream that he and James compete as a team.

Finally the rains stopped and the grounds slowly dried out. Randy leveled and plowed the arena and they were able to resume roping again.

At one of the weekly ropings, an Oklahoma cowboy named Rob Miller introduced himself to Randy. He was relocating to the northeast Texas area and wanted to know if Randy knew of any places for sale or rent where he could keep his horses.

"Don't know about any places right off, but I'm sure there are some," Randy replied, when asked.

"Well, we're going to have to find something fast. We can stay in a motel until we locate something, but I've got to find a place to keep my horses."

"You can keep your horses here... and you're welcome to stay here until you can find a place," Randy said.

"I hate to put you out."

"No problem at all. Glad to help. I've had more than my share of help lately. About time I repaid some of it."

"I'd appreciate it... if you're sure it's all right."

"It's just my son, Brett, and me, so we can make it with no problem."

After Rob, his wife, and a young daughter settled in, Rob began to help Randy with the steers and ropings.

He also began to work with Randy on roping. Rob would lope around the arena and Randy would ride up behind him on Watch Joe roping the back legs of Rob's horse. Rob helped by telling him what he was doing right and what he was doing wrong. Randy learned a lot from those practice sessions.

After a few days of trailing Rob's horse, Randy decided it was time to rope a steer. There were several local cowboys around that day to help and watch, and Randy felt as he had right before he got down on a bareback bronc. His mouth felt like cotton looked, and he had butterflies in his stomach.

Rob saddled Watch Joe, helped Randy into the saddle and handed him his heeling rope.

"You ready?" Rob asked, looking at Randy.

"Man, I've been waiting almost two years for this. I'm as ready as a man can get," Randy replied, coiling his rope.

"I'll get my horse and meet you in the arena," Rob said, as he walked toward the barn.

The other cowboys had already loaded the steers in the chute and put bonnets on them. They were sitting around the fence waiting as Randy rode through the arena gate.

"Steers ready and waiting," one of the cowboys shouted.

"I'll warm Watch Joe up," Randy replied, as he clucked to his willing horse and moved into a fast lope.

Watch Joe somehow sensed that this day was different from the others. He was more alert and his step was quicker.

Rob rode up next to Randy as they slowed to a walk.

"After I rope the steer, I'll just kind of stop him and then lead him off. That way you can work your horse in position a little better. What do you think?" Rob asked.

"Sounds good. But I don't want to get in the habit of going slow. You can't win anything going slow," Randy replied, his competitive spirit aroused.

"I'm with you," Rob said, smiling.

"Let's do it," Randy said, walking Watch Joe into the heeler side box. He turned his horse to face the steer as Rob rode into the header side and did the same.

Jay Sorrels, a young, stocky cowboy, positioned himself on top of the chute where he could open the gate. He turned his head so he could see Rob. The header would nod when he wanted the gateman to open the gate and let the steer run for the other end of the arena.

"Ready?" Rob asked, looking at Randy across the chute.

"Ready as I'll ever be," Randy replied, watching the steer.

Rob looked over at the steer to make sure he was straight

and ready to come out when the gate was opened. He held the reins and coiled slack in his left hand with the loop held in his right hand, away from the horse's side.

He glanced once more toward Randy to make sure he was ready, then he nodded his head for Jay to open the gate.

The gate flew open with the sound of metal crashing against metal and the steer lunged out. Rob leaned forward and his horse leapt from the box, heading for the steer. Randy held Watch Joe back for a split second, then released him. The sorrel leapt forward, slamming Randy hard against the back of the saddle. This was the first real test of the saddle. The horse had never thrown this much power at the saddle and Randy.

It was all a blur to Randy. As he became aware of dirt clods hitting him in the face, he saw Rob's horse quickly moving up behind the steer and Rob twirling the rope over his head. Watch Joe was pounding the ground with his ears pinned back against his head, heading for the steer's side. Randy instinctively checked Watch Joe by applying a small amount of pressure to the reins.

Then he saw the rope leave Rob's hand and snake toward the steer's horns. As the loop settled around the horns, Rob pulled the slack and quickly wrapped the rope around the saddle horn. Then, without hesitation, the steer's head came up from the pull on the rope and the steer began to turn away. Rob was leading the steer to the left of Randy, giving him a chance to rope the back legs.

Randy twirled his rope over his head and looked for the steer's back legs. The legs moved forward, then extended backward. Seeing an opportunity, Randy threw the loop hard toward the rapidly disappearing legs.

The loop went into the sand and appeared to encircle both of the steer's back legs, but as Randy attempted to pull the slack out of the rope, the steer stepped away and Randy held an empty rope.

Rob stopped leading the steer as soon as he saw that Randy had thrown his loop. After releasing the steer, Rob walked up to Randy.

"Well, that was a good loop. He just stepped out of it before you could pull your slack," Rob said, looking at Randy coil his rope.

"Man, I forgot how fast things get. That old steer was heading to the other end," Randy commented.

"How did the saddle feel?"

"When Watch Joe took off it really slammed me against the back. It almost knocked the breath out of me. And it seemed like I was having a hard time seeing the steer's back legs. I believe the saddle back is leaning too far back and throwing me where I can't see good right down in front of the horse," Randy said as they walked back to the chute.

"Ready for another?" Jay asked, as Randy and Rob walked their horses back to the chute.

"I'm ready, if you are," Rob said, looking at Randy.

"Man, I've been looking forward to this day for two years. You bet I'm ready. Just keep turning them suckers out and we'll keep roping 'em," Randy replied, backing his horse into the box.

One hour and twelve steers later, Randy said he had better quit for a while.

"You all right?" Rob asked.

"Yeah... but my right arm feels like it's going to fall off," Randy said, rubbing his right arm and shoulder.

"You did good," Rob said.

"It wasn't good, but it's a start."

Randy sat on his horse watching while the other cowboys roped. In his mind he went through the motions as one by one they headed and heeled the steers. He saw himself diving behind the steer, quickly throwing a snappy loop encircling both back legs, and going to the saddle horn with a fast dally. If he was to compete professionally, this was the way he had to do it. And somehow he would. Whatever it took, he would do it.

For the first several weeks after Randy started roping, he roped mostly with Rob Miller, Jay Sorrels, and Stanley Giles. Then James came over one afternoon to watch them rope.

Randy rode up to where James was standing by the fence.

"How're you doing?" Randy asked.

"About as well as can be expected under the circumstances," James replied, smiling.

"Want to head a couple for me?" Randy asked.

"Naw, I'll just watch."

"I can borrow a horse," Randy said, looking around.

"Well, I might rope one or two... it's been a while since I roped," James said, climbing over the fence.

A horse was offered, and, after adjusting the stirrup length to fit him, James stepped up.

Rob offered a coiled heading rope.

"It might fit you... it's a soft lay 7/16 scant."

"Thanks, it'll do fine," James replied, accepting the rope.

James backed the stocky bay horse back into the heading box while Randy backed Watch Joe into the heeling side. James glanced to see if Randy was in position.

"Ready?" James asked.

"Any time you are."

James nodded his head and the gate flew open. It had been over a year since James had roped but he threw a quick perfect loop and turned the steer for Randy. Randy swooped in as he had dreamed he could and picked up both back legs, a good run by anyone's standard.

After taking the ropes off the steer, James rode up to his smiling brother. "Felt pretty good, didn't it?" James said, smiling.

"Man, it was great. We can do it. We can make it rodeoing. All we have to do is work at it, be consistent and get our time down," Randy said, getting more and more excited over the prospect of returning to rodeo.

After everyone had gone and Rob and Brett were tending to the steers, Randy and James sat beneath a tree next to the arena. Neither spoke for several minutes.

"I've missed you," Randy said, turning to his brother.

"Me too," James replied, looking down at the ground.

"Becky and the kids went back to the coast," James said, without looking up.

"I was afraid of that."

"It's just one of those things."

"What happens next?" Randy asked.

"I don't know. I quit my job on the rig last week. I'm going to find a job around here."

Randy wasn't sure what to say. He knew his brother was hurting. James had been there for him when he was hurting. Now it was his turn.

"What can I do to help?" Randy asked.

"It'll all work out."

"Rob is planning on going to California within the next few weeks. Would you like to move back here until things get settled?"

"Thanks, but I'll stay where I'm at right now. Well, guess I'd better get along. Enjoyed the roping. We'll have to do it more often," James said, as he stood up.

"We need to get us a good heading horse and with a little practice we could rope with the best of them. What do you think?" Randy asked.

"Yeah, we sure could. Well… better go. See you later," James said, as he slapped his brother on the back. "Take care of yourself."

"I will. You do the same." Randy smiled, as he watched his brother walk slowly back to his truck and drive away.

That night Randy gave thanks for his brother's returning to be part of his life again. He had missed him more than anyone knew.

A couple of weeks later, Rob told Randy that he and his family would be moving to California. Randy was going out the door when Rob approached him.

"Randy, hold up a minute," Rob said.

Randy shut the door and turned to face Rob.

"What's up?" Randy asked.

"My brother called me about a job in California. We'll be leaving right away. I just wanted to thank you for letting us stay. Looks like it'll be a better deal for us out there."

"I'm the one that needs to be thankful. I'd still be roping the dummy steer if it hadn't been for you. I appreciate it, and I'll miss y'all," Randy said, offering his hand.

"Well, I'm glad I was able to help some. But I can't take any credit. You're going to make it. I'm convinced you can, and will, do whatever you want. I just hope you don't break your fool neck again," Rob said with a smile.

Soon it was just Randy and Brett again.

As word spread about Randy and all that he could do, he was more and more in demand as a speaker. He spoke to groups ranging from rehabilitation centers to civic clubs to schools. Randy never refused an invitation and was always eager to tell his story.

One particular visit was to the Greenville Christian Academy. The children were split into two groups. He would speak first to the elementary grades and then to those in middle to high school. Upon arriving, Randy went directly to assembly. He told the story of his life from the accident until the present time. Then he asked the children if they had any questions.

"What happened to the dog?" a little girl asked.

"He's fine. He still lives with me," Randy answered, smiling.

"Did you punish him for causing the accident?"

"No, I was just glad to be alive. Besides, he didn't cause the accident. I did."

"Will you ever walk again?" a small boy asked.

"If God wants me to."

"Have you given up thinking that God will perform a miracle?"

"No, if it is to be, God will make it happen. Until then, I need to do the best I can."

"Do you love God more now than you did before the accident?"

"I understand more about His love than I did before the accident. And yes, I do love God more now."

"Do you blame God for the accident and being paralyzed?"

Randy had to think about this question. The room became silent as he thought back to when he asked God why it had happened to him, and the times he thought God had forsaken him. Then he answered.

"Yes, I did blame God. But then I realized I did it to myself. God didn't tell me to drink alcohol and drive. We have to be responsible for our own actions."

For the first time since the accident, he had finally said out loud what he had been thinking and avoiding. If he hadn't been drinking alcohol, the accident might not have happened. He might not be paralyzed today.

The next group was the older children, and Randy made an even harder plea for not drinking and driving.

"You are at the age where you might want to try drugs and alcohol. My advice—no, my plea to you is, DON'T DO IT! Just look at me and remember how I got paralyzed. Please don't do drugs or alcohol... and for sure don't drink and drive."

James went to work at a western store in Greenville and he and Randy began making plans about how they would return to rodeo. One of the first things they needed was a professional heading horse for James. Randy already had

Watch Joe well on his way to being a top-notch heeling horse. Both men had the desire and determination to succeed. All they needed now was a horse and plenty of practice.

Chapter 13

In March of 1989, Randy's life changed drastically once more. He met Marilyn Leps and fell in love. Marilyn was a young widow with a beautiful little girl named Christina and a baby boy named Matthew.

The first time Randy met her, Marilyn was working at a local department store where Randy's Aunt Patsy worked.

After their first meeting, Aunt Patsy told Randy that Marilyn thought he was real nice and she had enjoyed meeting him. That was about all the encouragement Randy needed, and he asked Marilyn out. In the beginning they mostly went to dinner, or sometimes Randy would meet her at the mall and they would go to lunch.

Randy was hesitant at first. He wasn't sure if Marilyn was just being nice, or if she was really interested in him. But the more they talked and got to know each other, the more he liked and trusted her.

Marilyn was impressed with Randy's sincerity and approachable personality and was immediately drawn to him. She was able to look past Randy's obvious disabilities and see the real man. She saw a compassionate, fun-loving, dedicated, and determined person. It gave her pleasure just to be around him.

Their love and respect for each other grew stronger every day. It was as if they had known each other for years.

Randy was still trying to find a reputable maker of quality saddles to mass-produce his saddle. But so far he had had no luck. Then one day, as he was talking with James about getting his saddle built, James had an idea.

"The man who owns the western store where I work is one of the biggest saddle makers in the nation," James said. "If we approached him about building and marketing your saddle and could show him where he could profit, I'm willing to bet he'd do it."

"Why haven't you said something before now?" Randy asked.

"I'd thought about it, but I figured you would say something when you were ready."

"Well, I'm ready. When can I talk to him?"

"I'll set up an appointment to see him."

The following week James and Randy met with the owner.

When they arrived at the saddle company office, there was no wheelchair access.

"Well, it looks like we have a small problem," James said, as he pushed Randy up to the bottom of the steps.

"Is there any other way in?"

"Yeah, but there's just more steps. I'll carry you up and set you down on the top step and then get your wheelchair," James said, as he cupped his arms under his brother's legs and lifted Randy up.

There were only about ten steps but it seemed like fifty by the time James set Randy down.

The owner was expecting them, so they went right into

his office. After James introduced Randy, the brothers presented their proposal for building the saddle. Randy explained about the saddle, its benefits to the physically challenged, and its market potential.

There are millions of physically handicapped persons in the United States alone; untold millions in the rest of the world.

Randy explained that it was a difficult saddle to build. The one saddle they had built needed modifications to make it stronger and more functional. It would take expertise and a special saddle maker to provide a high-quality saddle.

James and Randy both stressed the importance of using quality-tested material, because a handicapped person using the saddle was depending on them to provide a safe, usable product.

After discussions, the owner agreed to build the saddle to Randy's specifications if he would help promote it, which both Randy and James agreed to do. They would incorporate all the modifications Randy proposed and Randy would get to try out the first saddle produced. (Randy Baties built the modified saddletree and still builds all of the trees.)

The owner fulfilled every obligation he had committed to throughout the term of the contract. And he later sponsored Randy and James in rodeo competition across the state.

Several different saddles were built and tested over the next few months before they settled on a final version. Then production of the saddle began.

James and Becky divorced, and shortly after, James fell in love and married. He and his wife, Judy, moved to a ranch not far from Randy.

James acquired a top-notch heading horse, and then he and Randy began roping in earnest. They practiced almost every day after James got off work at the western store.

There were days when James was tired and roping was the furthermost thing from his mind, but Randy would talk him into it. Randy was convinced they could be roping champions if they worked hard enough.

They started entering local jackpot ropings and began to win, but they were still not consistent enough to enter professional rodeos.

Randy stopped holding public ropings at the ranch but continued to keep steers for him and James to practice with. They were both convinced that with more practice and seasoning they could win in professional rodeo.

One summer day, James got a call from Steve at the Horseman's Club in Greenville. He had several longhorn cows and calves he couldn't pen and he wanted James and Randy to rope them.

They trailered their horses over to Steve's place the next day. Randy hadn't done any pasture work since the accident, but he was looking forward to it. It would be another test for him and his saddle.

James kept reminding Randy that if the horse were to fall with him strapped in the saddle, there was a good chance the horse would roll over on him. Randy understood the risk and accepted it.

There were washes and gullies throughout the place and those longhorn cows ran up, down, and through every one of them at least once. The brothers roped and penned a couple of the cows, then they went after the largest horned cow. She had a wide horn span and the points were sharp as knives.

They eased the big cow out into the open and after a short run James roped her. They were fairly close to a steel corral, so James attempted to lead the bellowing cow into the corral while Randy got behind her and kept her moving. Now this cow was hot, mad, and tired of being dragged, so, just as James led her into the corral, she lowered her horns and ran at James' horse. The horse froze instead of jumping out of the way, and when James went to kick him it was too late. The cow was almost upon them.

Randy saw the cow charge and quickly twirled his rope over his head, throwing a loop for the longhorn's back legs. The loop encircled her back legs and, with only a foot between her horns and the belly of James' horse, she hit the end of Randy's rope.

The impact jerked Watch Joe forward and slammed Randy against the high back of the saddle. This knocked the wind out of him and broke the saddle back. But he had saved James' horse from being gored, and possibly saved James from serious injury.

Now this madder-than-the-dickens cow was sprawled out on the ground bellowing and carrying on when Steve came into the corral.

As Steve squatted down next to the cow's head to take the rope off, Randy yelled at him.

"That ol' cow's mad at everything right now. I sure wouldn't take those ropes off just yet."

"These longhorns aren't bad cattle," Steve said, as he

pulled the ropes loose.

He had hardly got straightened up before she leapt to her feet and lunged at him. Steve ran for the fence, but he couldn't climb it. The corral was solid fence up to the top so there wasn't any way to get a toehold to climb it. About the time he looked over his shoulder, that longhorn cow just ran her horns up under his rear and tossed him completely over the fence. Then she turned around to find something else to take out her meanness on. Randy and James had made a quick exit through the gate and shut it behind them, leaving her to stand by herself, pawing and bellowing.

This incident caused several additional modifications to be made to the saddle. This time Randy felt he had the best design possible: it had been honest-to-goodness field-tested.

One of the first saddles Randy sold was to Kristi Koonsman, whom he had met at the Dallas Rehabilitation Institute in 1987. She had read an article about Randy and his saddle in a magazine, and called Randy. Her mother and father drove her from Hico, Texas, to Greenville so she could see the saddle for herself.

When Kristi saw the saddle and realized that there was a possibility she could ride a horse again, she was excited. Kristi had worked cattle on the family ranch and competed in barrel racing before her accident. The past months had been a nightmare for her.

The Koonsmans purchased the saddle and Kristi couldn't wait to ride. The next day an excited, thankful Kristi called Randy to tell him how well the saddle performed. She had already helped work cattle. It was as if she had been given life back.

A few months later, Randy contacted the Dallas Rehabilitation Institute about visiting and demonstrating the saddle. The DRI staff was very interested and invited him to visit the next week.

Randy contacted Kristi and invited her to go with him, an offer she enthusiastically accepted. If it could help just one person as it had helped her it would be worth the trip, she said.

Randy took one of the new saddles with him to DRI. The DRI staff was more enthusiastic about the saddle and its potential therapeutic value than were the patients. None of the patients were horse people and they couldn't see themselves riding a horse no matter how therapeutic it was. Most were concerned with how they were going to make a living and survive in a world designed for able-bodied people.

Randy told them that being able to ride again had made him feel as if he had regained his life and that it had been as important to feel good about himself as it was to physically recover from his injuries. Each person, he told them, has to recover both mentally and physically for his rehabilitation to be complete. And whether it was riding horses or participating in other activities, they could gradually do all the things they had done before. They just had to find different ways to do them.

Because they were in a wheelchair, he said, didn't mean life was over. He was still the same person. He still had the same dreams and goals. But now he just had to approach those dreams and goals from a different perspective.

Kristi explained what it meant for her to be able to ride again. She talked about herding cattle and participating in ranch activities. She had regained her confidence and her whole outlook had changed. She was looking forward to the future, because now she felt as if she had a future.

After the presentation, DRI staff members thanked Randy and Kristi for coming. They were both perfect examples of what rehabilitation was all about.

Chapter 14

It was January 1990 and Randy decided he would get a job until summer. The weather restricted his outdoor activities and he could certainly use the money.

He applied for a job working in the western store where James was working, and got it. It felt good to work again and helped build his confidence.

He seemed to heal both physically and mentally as every day passed. His weight was almost back to what it had been before the accident and he hadn't had an infection since his teeth had been fixed.

Randy and Marilyn continued to date, becoming constant companions. On March 5, 1990, one year after they had met, they were married and Randy accepted Christina and Matthew as his own children.

He now had a family that depended on him and it felt right. The healing process was almost complete.

Randy's saddle was now available and he needed to market it to get the message to the public. The saddle company began advertising the saddle in their catalogs and when Randy and James went to a roping there was interest from those attending. But Randy felt they needed high-visibility media coverage to get their message to people who could benefit from the saddle. Paralyzed and disabled people didn't usually come to team ropings, and that was the segment of the population Randy wanted to direct his message to.

The Greenville newspaper ran a feature article on Randy, James, and the special saddle. After that article, many feature articles were published statewide and, then later, nationally.

At every rodeo they attended, the news media was there, and Randy's and James' fame spread. As they gained more and more public recognition, sales for the saddle began to increase. A local televised horse show heard about them and did a feature that created more interest in the saddle. Then a syndicated statewide television show contacted Randy about doing a feature on him. They wanted to show him at the western store working, and him and James practicing roping. This would be to give the viewer insight about the saddle and how it was built. Then they would close the feature with Randy and James roping at Fort Worth at the Saturday night Professional Rodeo Cowboys Association rodeo.

The weather didn't cooperate, so instead of roping at the uncovered arena, they made arrangements to rope at a Greenville indoor arena.

Randy was contacted by a man who had been paralyzed from the waist down as a result of an industrial accident. He had been a team roper before the accident and had heard about Randy's saddle. Randy told him to be at the indoor arena on the day of the filming and he could try the saddle then.

Randy contacted the television show producer and told him it would add a new dimension to have this man try the saddle for the first time on the show. The director agreed.

The morning they were to meet with the filming crew, Randy and James got up early, loaded their horses and drove to the arena. The film crew was there when they pulled into the parking lot. They introduced themselves and outlined how they would like to do the interview and filming. Then as James unloaded and saddled the horses, filming began.

Randy looked around for the man who was supposed to meet him and try the saddle. He noticed a woman pushing a man in a wheelchair toward him. Randy wheeled himself to meet them.

"I'm Randy Bird," he said, extending his hand.

"Chuck Gleaves," the man answered, grasping Randy's hand with a firm grip.

"How long has it been since you were paralyzed?" Randy asked.

"About a year," Chuck quietly replied.

"It's been four years for me."

"How does this saddle work?"

"It's just like any other saddle, except it's got a high back and a wide belly band to hold you in. I've been roping for a couple of years."

"I'm looking forward to trying it. I sure miss riding and roping."

"I know how you feel. You were heeling before the accident, weren't you?" Randy asked.

"Yeah, but I haven't picked up a rope since I was hurt. Didn't seem like there was any reason to," Chuck said, looking at the ground.

"Well, there's reason to now. If I can rope, you can, too."

The film crew was everywhere with their cameras and recording equipment. They recorded and filmed Randy's and Chuck's conversation.

Then it was time for Randy and James to rope. Randy was a little nervous as James lifted him up on Watch Joe. "You're going to have to go on a diet," James whispered as he lifted Randy up.

They roped several steers while the film crew recorded the action. Chuck watched every move Randy made, waiting for his opportunity to ride. Then it was time for Chuck to try out the saddle. Two of the cowboys who had come with Chuck lifted him up onto the saddle while Randy offered instructions and suggestions.

After riding around the arena getting used to the saddle, Chuck told Randy he thought he was as ready as he would ever be. Randy tried to tell him not to expect too much the first few times, that it would get better the more he roped. But Chuck was so excited he didn't hear a word Randy or anyone else said.

He backed Watch Joe into the heeler box while James backed his horse in the other side.

James glanced at Chuck, asking him if he was ready. Chuck nodded his head as he watched the steer. James nodded his head for the steer to be let out and the action began!

James quickly ran his horse behind the steer, roped the horns and led the steer off to the left. Chuck moved up behind the steer and threw his loop. He was too far away and missed, but he felt wonderful!

Chuck's eyes were alight with excitement as he rode

Watch Joe back into the roping box. This time Chuck moved up quickly, and when the loop settled around the steer's back legs, he let out a yell of joy. As he rode up to Randy, he was smiling from ear to ear.

"You got a sale! When can I get it?"

"It'll take a few weeks, but I'll hurry it along," Randy said, smiling.

As Chuck continued to rope one steer after another, his wife came over to Randy and put her arms around him.

"I can't thank you enough," she whispered, as tears ran down her face. "This is the first time he has smiled since the accident."

"He's going to make it. It'll just take time. Now he can get on with his life. He'll find that he can do just about anything he could ever do, it'll just be done a little different," Randy said, patting her arm.

The last part of the feature was to be filmed at the Fort Worth rodeo the following Saturday night.

Randy and James arrived early, as they usually did. It took a little longer for them to prepare than it did the other cowboys.

The television film crew was already set up and waiting when they arrived. The filming would have to be done as the action happened.

Randy and James were sitting on their horses behind the chutes, waiting for their turn to rope when their names were called over the loudspeaker.

"Well, here we go," James said, looking at Randy. "Let's show 'em how it's done."

"OK," Randy replied, as he reined Watch Joe through the

alley and into the bright lights of the arena.

As Randy and James entered the arena the announcer introduced them.

"Ladies and gentlemen, I want to direct your attention to the cowboy who just came into the arena. This man is my hero. If you will notice his saddle is not like the other cowboys' in this event. Randy Bird is paralyzed from the waist down. But he is here tonight to compete in the team roping with his brother, James Bird, just like the other contestants. I want you to give them a special Fort Worth, Texas, welcome."

The crowd immediately rose and gave Randy a standing ovation.

Randy and James were not successful that summer night; at least they didn't win the roping. But if success can be measured by courage and determination, Randy did win.

At the close of the interview Randy was asked about winning.

"How do you feel about not winning tonight?" the interviewer asked.

"Sometimes you win, and sometimes you lose. That's the way it is. This night we lost, but there's always another rodeo down the road. There's people that say to me, 'Randy, if you never win a rodeo, you're already a winner.' Well... maybe it's just the cowboy in me, but they can say what they please while I beat 'em and take their money."

The first professional rodeo they entered was in Huntsville, Texas. They had been practicing hard and entering local jackpots, so they believed it was time.

It was a three-day rodeo and the winning score would be

based on the fastest time from the three combined performances.

Randy and James were scheduled for the Sunday performance. During the drive to Huntsville, Randy told James everything felt right. This was the time they were going to win.

They were the second team to rope that night and by the time their names were called, they were feeling the pressure.

As they rode into the arena and the announcer made note of Randy and his special saddle, James turned to his brother.

"I'm just going to jump out and turn the steer quick as I can."

"I'll be there," Randy said, backing Watch Joe into the heelers box.

Randy took a deep breath just as James nodded for the steer.

The steer came out as if shot from a cannon and James didn't catch him until they were more than halfway down the arena. He threw a long loop then led the steer off to the left. Randy twirled his loop over his head and as soon as the steer turned, threw his loop at the steer's back legs. The loop whirled around both back legs and Randy made two wraps around the saddle horn, while James faced the steer. The flagman whipped the flag down to signal the run was complete and to stop the clock.

As Randy and James coiled their ropes, the announcer's voice boomed over the loudspeaker.

"Ladies and Gentlemen, before the Bird brothers roped I called attention to the fact that Randy is paralyzed and rides a saddle he specially designed. Well, give them cowboys an extra special hand, because they're our new leaders in the team roping event."

The crowd went wild.

They won the go-'round and placed seventh in the average. They had roped against some of the best PRCA ropers around and had hung tough. They could certainly hold their heads up. There would be other days... other rodeos. It would happen. Their time was coming.

Randy and James spoke to any group or function that asked—churches, schools, and civic clubs. Randy continued to visit rehabilitation centers and anyone else in need. But more than anything, hundreds of people were changing their perspective on handicapped persons because of their contact with Randy.

One of the functions Randy and James were invited to was the Special Equine Olympics held at Burleson, Texas. They presented trophies to the winners in each event and provided a demonstration of team roping and horsemanship. It was a day-long affair, so Randy and James and their families arrived early in the morning.

They were going to rope at Fort Worth that night, so it would be a long day. They usually didn't leave Fort Worth until after midnight and it was a good hour-and-a-half drive home.

It was an exciting day for the youngsters as they participated and competed in the various classes of horsemanship. But it was also exciting and enjoyable for James and Randy. They learned a lot about mentally and physically challenged children that day, and Randy vowed to learn even more.

It would be hard to express the enthusiasm and joy those kids experienced riding horses and just being around them. There is something about a horse that will bring a child or even an adult out of his shell when nothing else can. Randy could see more and more how his saddle could benefit people.

Randy and James talked with the kids and signed autographs as long as there was a kid wanting one.

When the last bus load of kids was getting ready to go, there was one little boy who stood holding Randy's hand. A woman walked up and put her hand on the little boy's shoulder.

"Eddie, we'd better go now."

Eddie didn't say anything; he just kept staring at Randy and holding his hand.

"Eddie, the bus is waiting. We have to go."

Eddie released Randy's hand and, looking over his shoulder at Randy, walked toward the bus with the woman. Then he jerked away from the woman and ran up to Randy. He grabbed his hand and said, "You're the greatest man alive." He released Randy's hand once more and ran back to the woman. She smiled at Randy as she took Eddie's hand in hers, and they disappeared onto the bus.

After seeing firsthand what horses can accomplish for both mentally and physically challenged children, Randy began reading every article and publication he could find on the subject. He found out there were several foundations and organizations throughout the nation that provide therapeutic horse-riding programs.

It had already been proven that adults and children with a range of disabilities including cerebral palsy, multiple sclerosis, spina bifida, muscular dystrophy, mental retardation, closed-head injury, and quadriplegia can significantly benefit from therapeutic horse riding.

Persons associated with horses benefit on a multi-sensory level. Riding is a unique form of exercise in that the rider is dealing with a living, breathing being. There is no machine that can duplicate the emotional and physical therapy given by a horse. For a person who has never walked, riding a horse gives the nearest simulation of walking. Also, for the physically disabled, riding is a means to achieve parity with able-bodied people, through being able to sit at eye level with them.

The more obvious benefits provided from horse riding are exercise, strengthening of weak muscles, relaxing of spastic muscles, development of coordination and balance, and a tremendous boost in morale and self-esteem.

Despite the benefits of riding programs for the disabled, the thing that stood out to Randy was that they still used standard western and English-style saddles. This meant that some able-bodied person had to walk beside the riders to assist them. Thus, they never had the feeling of being completely on their own.

Randy's therapeutic saddle could eliminate the need for someone having to walk beside the riders. This then would be the big marketing message: the saddle would help disabled riders gain parity with able-bodied riders. Once they were on a horse, they were in control. . . and to people with disabilities, that is important.

Randy and James went to every rodeo and jackpot roping within driving distance for the rest of the summer. Between working, practicing, rodeoing, and driving, they weren't getting much rest, nor were they spending any time with their families.

They were improving, but still not roping consistently and not winning at the professional rodeos.

At one of the local jackpot ropings, Randy and James were leading in the competition. It was coming down to the last steer. If they made a good time on the last steer they had it won. They backed their horses into the roping boxes, determined to win.

The gate opened and the steer leapt forward from the chute. James roped and turned the steer and almost at the same time Randy threw his heel loop and quickly dallied the rope around the saddle horn. But somehow the rope got over his thumb, pinning it against the saddle horn. James was leading the steer away and had no way of knowing Randy's thumb was in the rope.

The rope burned the flesh on Randy's right thumb to the bone as it zipped around the saddle horn. Randy quickly reached forward with his left hand and grabbed the rope together in front of the saddle horn, stopping the steer and releasing his thumb.

James rode up to Randy, not knowing what happened.

"I think we won," James said. Then he saw Randy's thumb.

"What happened?"

"Dropped a coil and got my thumb," Randy replied, in obvious pain.

Marilyn overheard someone say that Randy Bird had cut his thumb off, so she leapt over the fence and ran up to Randy, tears running down her face.

"Randy, what happened?" she shouted.

"It's all right now," Randy assured her. "I got my thumb caught, but it's all right."

They went to the horse trailer and James helped Randy into the truck.

"Let's get you to a hospital," Marilyn said, as soon as she saw his thumb.

"There isn't anything they can do. The rope just burnt away the flesh. The bone's not broke. It's just going to take time to heal."

And take time it did. Even after the tissue healed, it took weeks to get to where he could move it. Even to this day when he goes to the horn to dally, he thinks about it. It's not something easily forgotten.

As the summer drew to a close, the grueling schedule began to take its toll on both Randy and James. They were juggling too many activities, and their family life was suffering. They were tired, irritable, and worn out physically and mentally, and Randy was still not completely up to speed after his thumb injury. During the time when Randy couldn't rope, James roped with other partners, but wasn't really able to click with any of them.

James finally decided to quit working at the western store and try rodeoing full time. He gave himself a couple of months to make it pay. If it didn't, he would quit rodeoing altogether.

When James told Randy about his decision, Randy was

afraid that his quitting the store would affect the contract he had with the owner to build the saddle. It might also affect Randy's working at the store. James assured him that his quitting wouldn't affect Randy's agreements. The only thing it would affect was the rodeo sponsorship.

After James quit, Randy continued to work at the western store for a while. Then he quit too, and he and the owner mutually agreed to dissolve the saddle contract, giving Randy all the rights to build the saddle himself.

After taking a few weeks off, Randy hired two experienced saddle makers and began making the Randy Bird Therapy Saddle himself. For the first time, he had full control over the quality and workmanship of the saddle. He immediately started receiving orders from all over the United States and even as far away as Australia.

The dream of producing the saddle and making it available to other handicapped persons around the world was alive and well.

Early one morning, James drove slowly up the gravel driveway leading to Randy's ranch home. He turned the engine off and sat staring at the steering wheel for several minutes before opening the door and stepping out. He shut the truck door and slowly walked to the front door.

Randy heard the truck coming and opened the front door as James walked up.

"Come on in," Randy said cheerfully, as he wheeled himself around and started to the kitchen. "I've got some coffee brewing."

Randy retrieved two cups from the counter top and sat

them down on the table.

"Good morning," James said, as he sat down.

"Hey, it can't be all that bad," Randy said, sensing that James was concerned over something.

"Yeah, it can be," James replied, staring at the floor.

"Well, out with it," Randy said, as he poured James a cup of coffee and handed it to him.

"I sold my horse," James said, looking at Randy.

"Why?"

"Matter of fact, I sold my horse, trailer, saddle, and even my lariat ropes. I don't have anything left that is associated with a horse or rodeo.

"I don't understand."

"Hey, it's simple. I've been running all over the country going to rodeos and spending money like it was going out of style. I'll bet I haven't spent two evenings at home in the past three months. It's time I quit for a while. Now that Amy and Cody are living with us it's not fair for me to be gone all the time and leave it up to Judy to take care of everything."

Randy was stunned. He looked at James in disbelief.

"We've had horses all our lives and rodeoed all our lives. How can you just quit?"

"Man, sometimes you have to do what you have to do."

"What about our plans of rodeoing together?" Randy asked.

"There's plenty of good headers that will rope with you."

"Yeah, but they're not my brother."

They both fell silent, lost in their individual thoughts.

"Well, I've got an interview for a job in Garland. I'll see you. Tell Brett hello for me." James said, as he stood up and pushed the chair under the table.

"Yeah, tell Judy and the kids hello for me," Randy responded, looking up at James.

James walked to the door, then turned around.

"This doesn't have anything to do with you. I think the past four years have just caught up with me. Man, I'm tired from the inside out. Take care of yourself."

"I will. You do the same."

James opened the door and walked to his truck without looking back.

Randy watched as his brother drove away.

Chapter 15

It was April 1991, the weather was warm, and Brett was playing baseball. At one of the baseball games, Randy met Travis Burney. Travis had been a lifetime horseman and roper, but had slowed down the past few years. The slowdown was due mostly to the day-after-day grind of competition and the travel involved.

Randy told Travis he needed someone he could work with to head steers for him. He also needed someone who could help him with his heeling. He didn't want to be only a token partner, he wanted to be able to pull his own weight and win.

Randy still blamed himself for the fact that he and James hadn't won more often than they had. He was determined to be as good as could possibly be.

The more Travis talked with Randy, the more excited he got. He liked Randy's enthusiasm and determination.

"I'll tell you what I'll do," Travis said. "I'll show you how to heel the right way. If you'll listen and do what I say, I'll head for you."

"I'll do my best," Randy replied, offering his hand.

"You got it."

"When can we start?" Randy asked.

"When can you get steers?"

"Next week."

"Then we'll start next week," Travis said, smiling.

Randy was excited. He had a feeling this was the beginning of something good.

Randy picked up the steers the following week and, after getting the arena in shape, called Travis. The work began.

During the week Randy worked at the saddle shop. He would hurry home in the afternoons and Travis would meet him.

Travis told him he needed to change his roping style completely to be able to compete professionally, and it wouldn't be easy. It would probably be easier if he had never roped before. Now he would have to retrain himself, and old habits were hard to break.

But Randy was a willing, determined student, and he worked hard. They started back with the roping dummy, working on style. Randy would sit on his horse roping the dummy's back legs while Travis commented on what he was doing right and what he was doing wrong.

After several days of dummy work, they began roping steers. At first Travis would rope and set the steers, giving Randy plenty of time to position himself. Then the pace quickened. By the end of May they were pushing hard.

Randy wanted to rope in the Louisiana State Team Roping Championship to be held at Monroe, Louisiana, in June. Now they had a goal. They were picking up speed and it was looking more and more as if they could compete and win, if they could just stay consistent.

Randy felt as if he needed that little extra sharpness to have the edge. So Travis suggested that his son head the steers while he stood out in the arena where Randy would rope and see if there was anything that would help him go faster.

After Travis saddled Watch Joe and helped Randy up, they walked to the arena.

"Now Randy, you have to concentrate on your roping. Just block out everything else. You know how to do it, so all you have to do is just go out there and do it," Travis said, patting Randy on the leg.

"I'll do it."

Randy backed his horse in the box. He felt confident. Finally it was coming together.

With the first steer out of the chute, Randy was a little behind and Travis told him.

"OK, I'll get my rope up faster and move in behind quicker," Randy said, building a loop and backing into the box.

Randy broke hard and the steer veered a little further to the right than most. Randy hit the right steel post a glancing blow with his right stirrup as he hurried to catch the steer. Watch Joe cut in behind the steer and Randy threw a perfect heel loop, catching both hind legs.

"Randy, that was great," Travis shouted, patting Randy on the leg. "Can you do it again?" he asked.

"You bet," Randy replied. "But put my stirrup back on; I lost it on the last run," he said, pointing to the stirrup lying about five feet from the box.

"How did that fall off?" Travis asked.

"When I came out I hit it against the corner post," Randy said, pointing at the post.

Travis quickly put the stirrup back on and put the rubber

band around Randy's boot to hold his foot in the stirrup.

"OK. You ready?" Travis asked.

"You bet."

Once more Randy quickly moved in position and roped both back legs. Then again and again. Each time Travis would slap him on the leg and ask him if he could do it again.

Then Randy's foot came out of the stirrup again and when Travis moved his leg something didn't look right. There was movement in his thigh area where there shouldn't be.

"Travis, something's wrong. I think my right leg is broken," Randy said, looking at the odd angle of his leg.

"Boy, some people will do anything to get out of work. Come on now. We've got lots of steers to rope yet. You're hot right now," Travis said, believing Randy was just kidding around.

"Hey, I'm serious. I believe my leg's broken."

"Don't kid around about something like that," Travis said, walking over to Randy.

"Pick up my foot carefully."

Travis picked up his foot slowly, and when he did it was evident his leg was broken at the thigh.

"My God, Randy... how could that have happened?"

"When I hit that post earlier, I suppose."

"Let's get you to the hospital."

They hurried to the barn while Travis' son ran to the house to tell Marilyn.

Marilyn ran from the house shouting, as Brett brought the truck to the barn.

"Oh, my God, Randy," Marilyn sobbed.

"It'll be all right. Everything is all right," Randy

assured her.

"What will we do?"

"We'll go to the hospital in Greenville and they'll put it in a cast and I'll come home. That's what we'll do," Randy said, calmly.

Brett drove them to the hospital while Travis and his son unsaddled the horses and put them away. Then they rushed to the hospital.

They took Randy right to the X-ray Department at the hospital and confirmed that he had indeed broken his leg. It was a clean break, which was the best kind to have if he had to break something. If it had somehow splintered and cut an artery, he could have bled to death roping steers and never known it until he passed out from loss of blood.

Randy thought they would be able to set his leg, put it in a cast, and then let him go home. They were in the emergency room waiting for the doctor to return when Travis came in. He was visibly shaken.

"Randy, I'm sorry. I had no idea you were hurt," Travis said, patting Randy.

"I didn't know either, so don't feel bad."

"What has the doctor said?" Travis asked.

"He said he'd be back in a few minutes and tell us what will have to be done. But I imagine they'll set and cast it and I can go home today. We'll still be able to rope at Monroe."

"Look, don't concern yourself with whether we rope or not. This is serious." Travis replied.

"Hey man, after what I've been through, this is a piece of cake," Randy said, smiling.

The doctor walked in and pulled a chair beside Randy.

"Well, we have two choices. We can put you in traction,

which will take a few weeks. Or we can surgically install a rod and you could possibly go home in a few days."

"I thought since it was a clean break you could just cast it and let me get on with my life."

"Nope, it don't work like that. It's going to take longer for the break to heal with you paralyzed. That's a fact of life."

"I'm planning on roping in a couple of weeks in Louisiana."

"You might be able to ride in two or three months. I'm sorry, but that's the way it is," the doctor said, patting Randy on the shoulder.

"Well, if you're sure they're my only alternatives, it'll have to be the surgery. I'm not going to lay around a hospital for two or three weeks," Randy said, looking at Marilyn.

Marilyn had been holding Randy's hand ever since they arrived. She was terrified.

"It'll be all right," Randy said to Marilyn, smiling.

Marilyn was trembling. She felt that, at any moment, she would begin to shake uncontrollably.

"When will you do the surgery?" Randy asked.

"In the morning. We'll do all the pre-operative testing this afternoon and get you in surgery early tomorrow. I'll see you before surgery and explain the procedure."

"All right. I'll see you in the morning," Randy said, as the doctor left the room.

"Randy, we're going. I'll take care of the horses and steers until you are able," Travis said, standing in the doorway.

"I appreciate it, but Brett will be there to take care of them, won't you?" Randy replied, looking at Brett.

"Sure, no problem." Brett said, looking down at the floor.

"Well, we're going, so you take care," Travis said. "I'll see you tomorrow."

"No need in you having to hang around here tomorrow," Randy said, looking at Travis.

"I'll be here."

After Travis and his son left, Randy turned to Marilyn. Her eyes were swollen from crying and she was still squeezing his hand with all her might.

"Hey, I'm all right," Randy smiled. "This is just a minor setback. I'll be good as new in a few weeks. It's nothing to get concerned about."

Marilyn bent over and put her arms around Randy's neck, hugging him so tight she almost choked him.

Brett wasn't sure what to say, so he didn't say anything. It brought back memories that he had just as soon forget. He looked down at his father, then walked over and sat down.

"Much as I hate to, we have to let Mama and Pa know what happened," Randy said. "Maybe it would be better to call Pa first and let him tell Mama. Boy, is she going to be mad. She said if I got hurt riding a horse not to call her; she didn't want to hear about it. But I guess we'd better let her know," Randy said.

"I'll call Pa when they move you to a room," Marilyn said.

"There's no need in you hanging around here. You better get on home and tell Christina and Matthew that everything is all right. But before you go, maybe you better call Pa."

"I am not going anywhere. Brett can take the truck and take care of Christina and Matthew," Marilyn said sternly.

While Randy was being moved to a room, Marilyn called Pa. He also thought it would be better if he told Randy's mother. He told Marilyn he would be at the hospital in less than an hour.

Within two hours, the waiting room was filled with Randy's friends and relatives, wanting to know how he was doing and what had happened. The story was retold several times throughout the afternoon and evening.

Finally the nurse told everyone they had to leave and let Randy rest. She also convinced Marilyn to go home and get some sleep.

After everyone had gone and Randy was alone, he was able to let down. Up to now he had had to be strong and positive, but what he had said and how he felt were two different things. Being back in a hospital was something he had said would never happen again, and yet here he was. Looking up at a blank white ceiling with the smell of the hospital filling his nostrils brought back unpleasant memories, and his pulse quickened. He had to fight down the fear that threatened to engulf him by telling himself it was just a minor setback. He would be riding and roping in no time. He was still thinking positive thoughts when the medication took over and he drifted off to sleep.

The next thing he remembered was the nurse shaking him.

"Mr. Bird. Mr. Bird. We're going to take you to surgery. Do you hear me?"

"Yes, ma'am. I hear you. What time is it?" Randy asked, still groggy.

"It's six-thirty."

"The doctor said he would tell me about the surgery. Where is he?"

"He'll be here in just a few minutes to talk with you."

As they were rolling the gurney into the room, the doctor

walked in.

"Are you ready?" the doctor asked, sitting down next to Randy.

"Ready as I'll ever be," Randy smiled.

"What we're going to do is simply thread a rod through the bone and fasten it on both ends with screws. Sound simple enough?"

"Sounds fine to me. How long before I can ride again?"

"It'll take a few weeks to heal. Let's not worry too much about riding right now," he smiled.

"Hey, I was finally getting my timing down and we were getting ready to rope in Louisiana when this happened."

"It won't hold you back long. I'll guarantee you that much," the doctor said, as he patted Randy and smiled.

As they wheeled Randy to surgery, the doctor told him they were going to give him something to relax him some more.

Since he didn't have any feeling in his legs there was no need for anesthesia. He told Randy the procedure would take about three hours, and then after a short time in recovery, he could go back to his room.

Randy was alert throughout the surgery and the doctor explained everything he was doing.

"Randy, when we get through here this leg will be stronger than it was before you broke it."

"Well," Randy said, "How about just going ahead and putting a rod in the other one? I might just get up and walk out of here."

After spending three days in the hospital, Randy went home. After eight weeks, he was back riding Watch Joe. Within ten weeks, he was roping again.

Chapter 16

It was August 5, 1991. The Bird family was celebrating Christina's birthday when a truck pulled up in front of the house. A man dressed in jeans and a wide-brimmed cowboy hat stepped from the truck and walked slowly toward the front door, appearing to be unsure if he was at the right place.

Randy had seen the truck coming when it turned off the road and had wheeled himself to the front door. He opened the door as the man walked up on the porch.

The man smiled when he saw Randy.

"Wasn't sure I had the right place for a minute there. I've asked half a dozen people where you live and was beginning to think I'd never find you. My name is George Marshall. I'm from Tyler, Texas," he said, offering his hand to Randy.

Randy opened the screen door and wheeled outside, letting the door slam shut behind him.

"Randy Bird," he said, shaking his hand.

"Yeah, I know who you are, but I imagine you'd like to know who I am," George said, smiling. "Can you talk a few minutes?"

"We're having a birthday party for my daughter…"

"Oh, I'm sorry. Let me tell you real quick why I'm here.

Have you heard about the Super Bull Tour?"

"Yes."

"Well, I'm one of the guys that puts it on. And I'd like for you to be part of the tour beginning in December. I saw an article about you in the *Dallas Morning News* and I believe it would be great to have you participate."

"I don't think I could ride bulls just yet," Randy said, smiling.

"Oh no, nothing like that. We would work out some kind of a routine you could do on your horse. Something that would show off your riding ability. Just how much can you do on horseback?"

"Just about anything anyone else can do."

"That covers a lot... What if we had you stay in the arena during the bull riding and help push the bulls out after each ride. Could you do that?"

"I can rope a bull, but my horse isn't big enough to drag a bull off."

"You wouldn't have to drag the bulls. There'd be other mounted men there. I thought it might be a good way to show how well you can manage with your special saddle. But we'll do something. The main thing is to show people what you can do. I believe I can get a sponsor—maybe someone like the National Paralysis Foundation. But if I can't, I'll sponsor you myself."

Randy was startled by the man's offer. He recalled a vision he had while attending a rodeo at Belton, Texas, a year ago. This was what had happened: After he and James had pulled into the rodeo grounds, Randy sensed that he should ride his horse into the arena by himself. James saddled Watch Joe and helped Randy on. Then Randy rode into the arena.

Several people were riding around the arena warming up their horses when Randy rode in. He walked Watch Joe to the middle and stopped. It was then that he had a brief but very detailed vision.

He saw himself riding up to a stage at one end of an arena, dismounting, and walking up to a microphone. He looked out at a large audience and said softly: "This is the power of God."

The vision was over as quickly as it had come. He became aware that the arena was completely empty—he was standing alone.

"Would you be interested?" George asked, breaking the silence and bringing Randy back to the conversation.

"Sure... sure I would," Randy replied.

The temperature was around 100 degrees, but Randy felt a cold chill go up the back of his neck.

"Would you be able to show me what you can do on a horse? I know you can't today. But would you be able to if I came back?"

"I broke my leg a few weeks ago. It'll be fine in a couple of weeks. Then I wouldn't mind at all."

"That would be just fine. I just wanted to know your capabilities so we could figure out what sort of routine we would want to do."

"Once I'm on that horse I can do just about anything anyone else can."

"The best I could understand from the article is that you are paralyzed from the waist down. And that you have built a special saddle and steer rope."

"That's about it," Randy said, smiling.

"That's pretty remarkable. And that's why I want you to be part of the Super Bull Tour. You'll have exposure to 150,000 people all over the Southwest. Not only will they be able to hear your story, they will see you perform. Just think about what it could do for the confidence of other disabled people. And it will show the non-disabled that just because you have physical limitations, it doesn't mean life is over. Man, it will be just great."

"When will it start? And how long will it take?" Randy asked, somewhat overwhelmed.

"The first performance will be December 31, 1991, in the Hemisfair in San Antonio, Texas. And it looks like the finals will be in Fort Worth, Texas, on April 4, 1992. There will be approximately thirteen cities with two performances at each location. We'll have fifty bull riders at each performance and there will be a country and western singer or group after the bull riding. Maybe between the bull riding and the entertainment, you could come out and ride while the announcer tells your story. That will be good. We'll come up with something. What do you think?"

"Can I talk to my wife before giving you an answer?"

"Sure. But let me know pretty quick. I want to find a sponsor and start making plans. Also I would like to use some of the feature articles written about you to show potential sponsors. If that's all right with you?"

"Yeah, that would be just fine. I even have several videos that show me riding and roping."

"That's great. Well, I've taken you away from your daughter's birthday party too long. Here's my card. Call me soon as you can and we'll work out the details," George said, offering Randy his hand. Randy watched as George returned to his truck and drove away. Then he wheeled around and went back into the house.

"Who was that?" Marilyn asked.

"You would never guess what he wanted. Not in a million years," Randy replied, with a broad smile.

"Don't make me guess. Tell me."

"He's from Tyler and he's one of the guys that puts the Super Bull on around the country," Randy said, handing the business card to Marilyn. "He wants me to go on the tour this winter. Can you believe that?"

"What would you do? Is it dangerous?"

"I wouldn't be riding any bulls, if that's what you're worried about," Randy said, smiling.

"Where all would you be going?"

"He said they travel all over the Southwest. It's held in an indoor arena. The first one is going to be at the Hemisfair in San Antonio. Sounds exciting, and think of the publicity I can get for my saddle. And maybe, in some small way, I can help other people with disabilities. Maybe I can even visit with rehabilitation centers and hospitals in the places where we go."

"Will they pay for your expenses?"

"I suppose. Well, they would have to. It will be expensive hauling a horse around the country. He said they would get a sponsor. So I suppose the sponsor would pay for expenses. I told him I'd get back to him soon as I talked to you about it."

"Well, it's up to you. But whatever you decide, please be careful. You're not healed from the last accident. Also it sounds like a lot of travel. How would you handle that?"

"I imagine Travis would go with me. And I would just

have to adjust to being on the road. There are a few motels that have rooms for the handicapped. If I can't find a handicapped room, I'll just have to make do. It won't be easy."

"Sounds like you have already decided," Marilyn said, smiling.

"If it's all right with you."

"It's all right with me. I just want you to be careful and don't get yourself hurt again," she said, putting her arms around her husband.

Randy called George Marshall the next day and told him he would go on the tour. George was almost as excited as Randy. They talked more about the tour and what Randy could do during the performance. George was going to contact potential sponsors and get back to Randy within the next two weeks.

Randy contacted Travis to see if he would travel with him. He had to have somebody accompany him. He would need someone to saddle and care for Watch Joe. And there were things that could go wrong on a long road trip. His truck could break down along some desolate stretch of road, or he could have a flat. What if he got sick away from home?

Randy still had fears of the unknown. How would he react to stressful situations? He hadn't been sick in several months and the severe shakes had all but disappeared. But still he was concerned that it could all return at any time. That possibility was always in the back of his mind. He was never completely relaxed when he was away from home.

Randy drove over to Travis' to talk. As he drove up, Travis

came out to meet him.

"What brings you out and about?" Travis asked, smiling as he leaned against the truck.

"Need to talk with you about something."

"All right, talk."

"A fellow by the name of George Marshall came by the other day and wants me to perform in the Super Bull Tour. Have you heard about it?"

"Sure have. But do you think you're up to riding bulls? You might ought to let your leg heal before you break your neck, don't you think?" Travis said, smiling.

"George said he would have me ride in the arena and push the bull out after a ride, or maybe just make up some routine I could do in between bull-riding segments. The plan now is to have fifty bull riders every night. There would be two performances at each location, and in between the fifty bull rides there would be an intermission. That might be a good time for me to ride around the arena while the announcer tells my story."

"Sounds good. You could get publicity for your saddle and show people firsthand that life isn't over just because a person is paralyzed."

"Exactly. Can you go with me?"

"What would I do?"

"Help with Watch Joe and baby-sit me," Randy said, smiling. "And maybe we could work out some kind of a roping routine where you could head a steer for me to heel."

"Sure, I'll go."

"Great. I'll know more about what will happen and when in the next couple of weeks. The first performance will be at San Antonio, December 31."

Randy felt better about going now that he knew Travis would be with him.

He began preparing for the tour. He built a new fancy saddle with all silver trim and embossed with RANDY BIRD THERAPY SADDLES across the saddle cantle in red, white, and blue lettering. If he was going to show his therapy saddle to thousands of people, he wanted it to look good.

It had been ten weeks since he broke his leg and Randy felt it was time to ride again. It had been hard to wait. Since he couldn't feel any pain from the break, it seemed as if he should have been able to ride before now. But he knew that, even though there was no pain, the leg still had to heal.

Travis came over to help him one fall day. "Sure you're ready for this?" Travis asked, as he saddled Watch Joe.

"Ready as I'll ever be," Randy replied, sitting in his wheelchair watching Travis.

"Does it bother you thinking about getting hurt again?"

"I try not to think about it. But I do sometimes."

"Is your leg healed?"

"The doctor said it was. But he also said not to stress it. I don't know what he means by stressing it. I sure ain't going to run no footraces or do any jumping. And I don't have any plans on banging it against the fence. So what the heck. I'm getting tired of being short. I want to get back on my horse and be tall again," Randy said, smiling.

Travis lifted Randy up on his horse and moved back. Randy strapped himself in the saddle, pulling the nylon band tight as Travis attached the rubber bands over Randy's boots and each stirrup.

Randy adjusted the bridle reins then leaned forward as far as he could to cue Watch Joe to move off in a walk. No one had ridden Watch Joe since the accident, but he walked off as if he had been ridden every day. Randy walked him around the arena a few times then he leaned forward and clucked his tongue, giving Watch Joe the cue to move into a lope.

At first Randy felt a little apprehensive, but the more he rode, the more his confidence returned. After a few rounds he pushed Watch Joe into an all-out run then pulled back on the reins into a dirt-throwing, sliding stop.

"Man, that felt good," Randy said, with a wide grin, as he rode up to Travis.

"Looked good," Travis replied.

"Give me a few days on the roping dummy and I'll be ready to start roping steers again."

"Take as long as you need. We're not in any hurry."

"I am. It seems like every time I'm just about to make it, something happens. This time we're going to win."

George Marshall contacted Randy, telling him that the National Paralysis Foundation would sponsor him. Randy would be a spokesman for the Foundation. Randy and George would meet with Kent Walthrop, the head of the Foundation in Fort Worth, and work out the details.

Now that it was settled that Randy would go on tour, he and Travis began roping again. But this time Randy was a little more careful about hitting the fence post. He didn't need any more injuries. He had had enough injuries to last a lifetime.

Chapter 17

Randy decided to leave early on the morning of December 31, so he and Travis didn't have to be in a hurry to drive to San Antonio. This would be the first Super Bull performance of the 1991–1992 winter tour. He kept telling himself he wasn't apprehensive, but he finally admitted that he was.

George Marshall still wasn't sure just what Randy was going to do at the performance. They wanted him to be on horseback in the arena and assist in moving the bulls out of the arena after a bull ride.

The plan, as Randy understood it, was that the arena would be divided; one part would be for bull riding and the other would be set with a stage for the country and western vocal group. There would be two segments of bull riding each night, with twenty-five rides during each segment. After the bull riding, a vocal group or an individual country and western singer would perform.

With the arena divided, Randy thought, it didn't seem there would be enough room to maneuver a horse around. If one of those two-thousand-pound bulls got after him, there wouldn't be any place to get away. But it wasn't up to him. He would just have to wait and see.

He thought to himself that he had seemed to do a lot of

waiting and seeing during the years since the accident. He was learning more and more to be patient, but he never really enjoyed it.

When he and Travis pulled into the Hemisfair parking lot, people were everywhere and trucks with trailers were pulling in and out of the building. Randy could feel his throat tighten as the activity around him intensified.

He still had a fear of being in a crowd. When he was home, he knew what to expect; he had control. Now, he didn't. But he was here and he had to see it through, he thought, as he guided the truck and horse trailer to a parking space.

"Well, we're here," Randy said, as he turned the engine off and set the emergency brake.

"We sure are. I suppose we ought to find out where we're supposed to put the horses before we unload them," Travis said, stepping out of the truck cab.

"I suppose. You know, this all sounded like a pretty good deal when we were talking about it. But I'm not so sure now."

"Hey, it's like anything you do. It might be a little strange and different at first, but after a couple of times it'll be old hat," Travis said, smiling. "I'll unload the wheelchair and help you down."

They finally found a door leading into the arena and Travis pushed Randy to where they could see inside. The steel partitions were already in place for the bull riding and the area was small—too small for a couple of horses and a bull, Randy thought, especially a bull that's already mad and ready to take it out on the first cowboy or horse he can get at.

"Man, there's not much room to maneuver in there,"

Randy commented more to himself than Travis.

"Not much," Travis agreed.

As the crowd began filing in and the noise intensified, Randy could feel himself tightening up more and more. It seemed the walls were closing in on him.

It was cold but he began to sweat. He was just getting ready to ask Travis to go outside when George Marshall walked up.

"See y'all made it," George said, as he offered his hand first to Randy then Travis.

"Yeah, it wasn't a bad drive. We got here about two hours ago."

"Randy, we're going to have to do something other than have you riding in the arena and pushing out bulls. There's not enough room for you to move around in case a bull gets after you," George said.

"It is kind of small," Randy agreed.

"What I think we'll do is have you ride your horse into the arena between bull-riding segments. You can work up a routine that'll take about ten minutes. While you're in the arena we'll have the announcer tell a little about you, your accident, and about the saddle. Also, we'll introduce you as the National Paralysis Foundation representative. What do you think about that?" George asked.

"Hey, whatever. Sounds all right to me."

"I'll have the announcer get with you. He's familiar with your story, but you'll need to fill him in on the details. Will that be all right with you?"

"Sure."

After talking to the announcer, Randy and Travis talked about what Randy could do for ten minutes. They decided that Randy, still in his wheelchair, would make an appearance in the arena. Then Travis would lead Watch Joe in and help Randy up onto the horse. Randy would walk Watch Joe around the arena a couple of times and then cue him into a lope. After a few rounds and a couple of figure-eights, he would push Watch Joe into an all-out run, then slide him up to one side of the arena, then to the other.

They decided to leave the horses in the trailer until it was time to saddle Watch Joe. Travis wouldn't need to saddle his horse after all.

It was almost time for the bull riding to start so Randy and Travis found a place to watch along the side of the arena but away from the bucking chutes.

The Hemisfair hadn't been designed for rodeo, so the portable pens and chutes had been trucked in and set up where the spectators were well away from the arena fence— a safety precaution in case some bull rammed his horns through the fence at an unsuspecting spectator.

As he sat and watched the events, Randy would glance up at the crowd from time to time and think about riding in front of them. It almost left him breathless. He would be by himself out there and he thought about everything that could happen. What if he fell off, or Watch Joe fell? What if he just looked stupid? That was the worst of all. What if he just looked like some paralyzed person trying to act like a normal person and ended up only looking stupid?

"Man, I wish I was home," he thought to himself.

After a few of the bull rides, Randy moved back from the fence. He was going over in his mind what he might do, when someone shouted that a bull had jumped the arena fence.

He quickly glanced around and didn't see a bull. There were people running in every direction and several cowboys and spectators jumped up on the steel partitions. About the time he decided to wheel himself toward the fence, he saw a bull dart into the hallway that led up into the spectator seats.

Soon the bull appeared in an adjoining hallway and took an exit back into the space between the arena fence and the permanent wall—right in the area where Randy was.

The bull stopped, faced Randy, bellowed, and pawed the ground as Randy wheeled around. Randy propelled himself with all his strength as he and Travis scurried toward the arena fence as the bull charged. Then, just as quickly, the enraged bull changed direction and ran back to where he had come from, ultimately going into the trailer that was used to transport him.

During all the excitement, Randy had wheeled next to the arena fence. After glancing over his shoulder and seeing that the bull had gone, he gave an enormous sigh of relief.

But just as he thought the danger had passed, an hysterical woman who thought the bull was still charging, saw Randy in the wheelchair. She reached down from the fence where she was perched, knocked Randy's hat off his head, and, grabbing a handful of his hair, attempted to pull him up to the safety of the fence.

In her attempts to lift Randy by the hair, she managed to bang his face against the steel fence and rip a fair-sized handful of hair from his head.

"Ma'am, ma'am, the bull's gone. Let go of my hair," Randy pleaded.

The lady finally stopped pulling on Randy's hair but kept shouting, "I thought the bull was going to kill you."

"I'm fine, ma'am, thank you." Randy said, attempting to locate his hat as he rubbed his head.

Travis retrieved Randy's hat and, after brushing the sand off, handed it to him.

"Man, I don't know who that lady is, but she dang near killed me. I'd have been better off taking my chances with the bull," Randy said, still rubbing his head.

As the intermission between the two bull-riding segments drew closer, Travis saddled Watch Joe and led him to the arena entrance.

While the bulls bucked one after another, Randy went over and over in his mind what he was going to do. But when he heard the announcer begin to introduce him, he forgot everything.

The announcer's voice boomed over the loudspeakers as George and Travis pushed Randy into the arena.

"Ladies and gentlemen, we've talked about champions tonight and our special guest this evening, representing the National Paralysis Foundation, is a true champion cowboy."

As the announcer continued, Travis and George helped Randy into the saddle. Randy adjusted the belly band as Travis fastened the rubber bands around Randy's boots and stirrups.

As George and Travis stood back, Randy cued Watch Joe into a lope, sliding him to a stop in the middle of the arena. He removed his hat and waved it high over his head as the announcer continued the introduction.

"Ladies and gentlemen, say hello to Randy Bird from

Quinlan, Texas. Randy is the only professional paraplegic cowboy in the world. With his heading partner, Travis Birney, he competes in the team roping event."

Randy glanced up at the crowd noticing that some were watching but most were unconcerned.

He cued Watch Joe into an extended lope, then reined the sorrel into a few figure-eights.

"Makes it look easy, doesn't he, ladies and gentlemen?" the announcer asked. "Randy almost lost his life in 1986 in a terrible automobile accident and was paralyzed from his waist down as you can see. He lost the use of his legs and was told he would never ride a horse again. But, in the tradition of cowboys past, he designed and built the Randy Bird Therapy Saddle. That's the saddle Randy is riding tonight. Randy has not only overcome his disability—he is a winner in every sense of the word."

A quick upward glance at the crowd showed Randy more people were watching. Then he cued Watch Joe into an all-out run, sliding him to a dirt-throwing stop as he removed his hat and waved it high above his head to the crowd.

The entire audience was on its feet. The applause was deafening.

He wheeled Watch Joe around and after a wide-open run around the arena slid to a stop facing the opposite side of the arena.

"Ladies and gentlemen... Randy Bird from Quinlan, Texas, a true champion of champions," the announcer shouted as Randy rode from the arena.

By now the bull-riding cowboys had come out from behind the bucking chutes to watch and they joined in with the crowd cheering Randy on. There were more than just a few with tears in their eyes.

The applause continued even after Randy had left the arena.

Randy rode up to Travis and stopped.

"I didn't look stupid, did I?" Randy asked, looking down at Travis.

"Nope, you didn't look stupid," Travis said, rubbing his eyes.

One by one the cowboys walked up and congratulated Randy. At last he felt as if he were one of them again, not just a paralyzed person trying to be a cowboy, but a cowboy who just happened to be paralyzed.

Chapter 18

After several performances at cities all over the Southwest, Randy began to feel more comfortable with the crowds and his performance. He began setting up a booth before the performances and distributing literature about paralysis provided by the National Paralysis Foundation.

He talked with handicapped and non-handicapped persons alike, answering questions and offering encouragement. It was this exposure that helped Randy overcome many of his fears and become more self-confident. In helping others he was helping himself.

His next performance was to be at Ardmore, Oklahoma, on January 17 and 18. By the time Randy was getting ready Friday morning, January 17, the weatherman was forecasting snow for the weekend in northern Texas and Oklahoma. Bad road conditions are always a concern when you're traveling, but when you're pulling a horse trailer, it's even more of a concern.

To make matters worse, Travis called a few minutes later to tell Randy he was sick with the flu and couldn't go with him on the trip.

Randy made several phone calls to local bull riders who were planning on going to Ardmore and a young cowboy named Jeff Montgomery agreed to accompany him. Jeff had gone with Randy on other occasions but he was going to another rodeo after the weekend Super Bull performances and wouldn't be able to come home with him.

Before the accident Randy had pulled horse trailers in all kinds of inclement weather and he could do it now. At least that is what he told Marilyn. He sounded more confident than he was.

The weather was cold and damp when Randy pulled onto the interstate highway in Greenville. He got an early start to allow plenty of time just in case they hit bad weather. But the trip to Ardmore went well on dry highway.

By now Randy had a standard routine after arrival. He would first make sure Watch Joe was fed and taken care of. (Most of the time Watch Joe had to stay in the trailer, but there were some places where stalls were available.) When his horse was taken care of, he would set up his booth.

After the bull riding started he would make his way down to the arena fence and watch. The cowboys who were competing would drop by and talk with him between bull rides.

Since Randy watched all the bulls bucking week after week, he got to know how each one bucked. It didn't take the cowboys long to figure out that Randy was a valuable source of information. So a lot of their talking was to find out what the bull that they had drawn for the performance was likely to do. Knowing the bull's moves could help them prepare mentally for the ride and know what to expect.

Randy had been acquainted with most of the cowboys before the accident, but he became acquainted with many more through the Super Bull competition. He was beginning to feel part of the rodeo.

One evening, Randy was watching the bull riding when a young cowboy caught his hand in his bull rope. The bull rope is a pleated rope that encircles the bull right behind his front legs, runs through a loop, and is pulled tight over the shoulder. Then the bull rider wraps the end, or the tail, of the rope over and around his hand. The only thing that holds the rope tight around the bull is the cowboy's grip.

Normally, when a cowboy releases his grip on the bull rope he is thrown clear of the bull. But sometimes when a bull bucks a cowboy off, the rope tightens around the cowboy's hand or wrist and becomes hung up. This is what happened to this young cowboy.

When the bull went spinning from under the cowboy, the momentum jerked him forward. The young cowboy hit his head against the bull's, and he was knocked unconscious.

The bull continued to spin as the cowboy was thrown around like a limp dishrag. Immediately, both bull-fighting clowns dashed to the spinning bull in an attempt to rescue the cowboy as the crowd leapt to its feet. The clowns tried to unwrap the rope from the cowboy's hand, only to be swatted and tossed aside by the bucking and spinning bull.

Randy watched as the clowns made one attempt after another to free the unconscious cowboy only to be butted away or stepped on by the enraged bull.

Then without warning the rope finally loosened and the cowboy sailed across the arena, landing with a sickening thud in the sandy arena.

The clowns darted and leapt in front of the bull in an attempt to keep his attention on them and not on the fallen cowboy, while paramedics and other cowboys ran to help the young man without regard for the enraged bull.

As Randy helplessly watched through the steel rods of the arena fence, a man leapt the fence and ran across the arena to where the young man was being attended.

Then a woman hurried up to the fence, wringing her hands as tears streamed down her face.

Randy looked up at the woman and somehow he knew this was the young man's mother.

"Ma'am, that's your son, isn't it?" Randy said, reaching out for her hand.

"Yes," she replied, in a shaky voice.

"Ma'am, do you want me to pray for him?"

"Yes, yes, please," she said, looking down at Randy.

Randy prayed for the young man while his mother sobbed uncontrollably.

Then, as Randy finished his prayer and glanced up, the cowboy was helped to his feet. After shaking his head a couple of times, he walked away under his own power.

Another cowboy handed the young man his hat, and, after slapping it against his leg to knock the sand off, he stuck it down on his head and smiled.

The audience gave the young cowboy a standing ovation as he disappeared behind the bucking chutes.

The woman turned to Randy, then reached down and hugged him so hard she was choking him.

"Thank you," she said, smiling, and then disappeared into the crowd to find her son.

The rest of the performance went without incident, but by Saturday night the weather had turned bad and it had begun to snow. Randy knew he would be by himself going home so he asked one of his cowboy friends to unsaddle Watch Joe and load the horse into the trailer. He decided to leave right after his performance, before the snow got any worse.

When he pulled onto the highway, snow was already piling up and the farther he went towards Texas, the heavier the snow accumulation.

This was just the kind of situation Randy had always dreaded, and he started thinking about everything that could go wrong.

What if the truck began to skid? The hand controls worked fine, but how would he react in a real emergency? What if the truck skidded off the road? He could freeze to death before help arrived. He couldn't just walk back to the road and hail someone down. What if the trailer jackknifed? And what if Watch Joe was thrown out? How could he help him? What if he slid into the other lane and hit some unsuspecting person head on?

Then he shook his head. "Hey, get hold of yourself," he thought. "Don't panic. You can do anything anyone else can. You've driven on ice and snow before and pulled horses all over the country. This isn't anything new. Just keep the speed constant, no quick movements. Got plenty of fuel," he continued, glancing at the truck's instruments.

He shifted in the seat to get into a more relaxed position. Then he turned the radio volume up so he could hear the weather report.

As he drove with the snow spitting against the windshield, he thought about the few years since the accident and the dramatic changes it had made in his life. He thought about Brett and how he had grown from a soft, irresponsible kid into a lean, self-confident young man.

He thought about Marilyn and how she had changed his life. And how much it had meant to have Christina and Matthew come into his life. If he had continued living as he had before the accident he might not have ever found Marilyn or enjoyed the closeness he and Brett shared.

As the miles passed, so did Randy's fears. He not only told himself he could take care of whatever happened, he believed it.

Randy changed that night on a snowy Oklahoma road... or maybe he had been changing all along and just realized it that night. He was no longer mentally dependent on anyone. There were some things he would always have to have physical help with, but lots of people had to do that. The difference was that he knew now he could handle whatever came along.

He thought about the young bull rider and his mother. Was that mother sent by God to stand by him so they could pray for the young man's recovery? And were their prayers answered, or was he just destined to recover? Randy felt prayer did make a difference.

He recalled when God had spoken to him after his accident and all of the blessings he had received since. He was finally healing. He was finally healing—mentally, physically, and spiritually.

Then, all of a sudden, he was aware that the highway was dry. It had stopped snowing.

The house was dark as Randy pulled slowly across the cattle guard and headed up the lane. It had been a long drive, but he had made it. And he had made it by himself. It was a good feeling.

He slowly backed the trailer beside the barn and turned the engine off. He opened the door and the rush of cold air made him shiver. Reaching behind the seat he pulled the wheelchair out and set it down beside the truck cab. Leaning over he snapped the wheels onto the axle and replaced the seat. Then he put his coat on and eased himself down from the truck cab into the wheelchair.

He wheeled himself to the back of the trailer and opened the trailer gate. Watch Joe turned around and walked out of the trailer beside Randy. As the horse stepped down from the trailer Randy reached for the lead rope. However, he leaned over too far. His wheelchair flipped up and slid out from under him, spilling Randy onto the gravel drive.

As he sat on the cold ground reaching for the wheelchair in the pitch dark, he laughed out loud at how he must look grappling around on the ground in the middle of the night. Then he scooted along, dragging the wheelchair until he got next to the truck cab. He finally reached the door handle and opened the door.

He attempted to pull himself up to where he could sit down in the wheelchair, but every time he would almost make it, the wheelchair would slide away.

Once when the wheelchair slipped from under him he fell completely under the high-built truck. He had to crawl and pull himself out.

After sitting back against the side of the truck out of breath, he began to laugh again.

"Well, I guess this is one of those times I'll have to get help," he said out loud.

He pulled himself up to where he could reach the truck horn and gave it a couple of sharp blasts.

Lights came on in the house almost immediately and Marilyn came flying out seconds later.

"Oh my God, Randy," she cried, kneeling down beside Randy.

"I'm fine," Randy smiled, holding her arm. "I just got down and couldn't get back in my chair. No problem," he laughed. "You had to be here to appreciate it."

"Here, let me help you up," Marilyn said, pulling on his arm.

"No, get Brett. You don't need to be pulling around on me."

"I'll be right back. Are you sure you're all right?"

"I'm sure. I've never been better."

Soon Brett came running out.

"Hey Dad, how did you get in that mess?" Brett asked, as he squatted down next to his father.

"It's a long story. I'll tell you all about it in the morning. Just help me back into the chair and find Watch Joe. He's wandering around out there somewhere."

Randy wheeled himself up the ramp where Marilyn was waiting with the door open.

"Are you sure you're not hurt?"

"I'm sure. Marilyn, I drove home from Ardmore in a snowstorm, by myself, and I made it. I'm going to be all right. I can do anything anybody else can do."

"I knew that all along," Marilyn said, smiling, as she hugged her husband.

Chapter 19

The 1991–1992 winter Super Bull Tour ended April 4, 1992, with the finals at the Cowtown Coliseum in Fort Worth, Texas. The Cowtown Coliseum has the distinction of being the site of the first indoor rodeo in the world. It seemed an appropriate place for the bull-riding finals.

Randy's family attended the last performance, so it was a special ending for Randy as well. He had mixed emotions about the tour ending. He was tired of the travel, but he had enjoyed the experience and the many people he had met and talked with in cities all over the Southwest.

The following Monday after the final Super Bull Tour performance, Randy got up early, feeling rested and looking forward to doing the many things that hadn't been getting done since the Super Bull Tour started in December. Marilyn and the children were hurrying around, getting ready for work and school. Randy was just going to relax for a while. It seemed as if he never had time any more to just sit and be able to think things through.

Randy wheeled himself to the front door as Marilyn approached. He pushed the front screen door open, holding it for Marilyn.

"What are you going to do with all your time since the

Super Bull Tour is over?" Marilyn asked, looking down at Randy.

"Well, I've got several saddles that need to be built, and there's work that needs to be done around here. Maybe Brett and I can rope more often, and I can help Matthew with his new pony. I'll have more opportunities to visit rehab centers. There's lots to do. I might just sit here on the front porch and watch the grass grow. There ain't no tellin' what I might do," he smiled.

"Sure, I can see you sitting watching grass grow. I have got to go to work. See you this afternoon," Marilyn said, bending over to hug and kiss Randy. "Love you."

"Love you, too," Randy replied, putting his arm around Marilyn's waist.

"Come on, Christina, and bring Matthew. I'm running late."

Christina hurried from the house, dragging a reluctant Matthew.

"Give me a hug before you go," Randy said, smiling as they hurried by.

Christina and Matthew paused just long enough to give Randy a quick hug then ran down the wooden ramp to the waiting car.

"See you two tonight," Randy said, waving.

"You going to be all right by yourself?" Marilyn said, as she walked down the ramp toward the car.

"Yep."

"Well, be careful."

"Careful is my middle name."

Marilyn laughed as she shook her head. She drove off down the lane, soon disappearing around the curve leading to the highway.

Brett came out and sat down next to his father.

"School will be out soon. What are you going to do this summer?" Randy asked, looking at Brett.

"Going to work."

"Think we can work in a little roping?" Randy asked, smiling.

"Sure, I ain't going to be working all the time," Brett agreed, returning the smile.

"Guess I'd better get on to school. See you this afternoon," Brett said, as he walked to his truck, waving.

"See you this afternoon. Be careful."

"I will be."

As Randy watched Brett disappear down the road, he thought about how much difference a few years make in a child's life. He remembered the short, chubby boy Brett had been and how, in a few short years, he had become a responsible, mature young man.

It was unbelievable, too, how Matthew and Christina had grown. Christina would be a young lady before they knew it and you could almost see Matthew growing.

Randy looked out across the green pasture. Everything was beginning to bloom and turn a brilliant, lush green. Trees were leafing out more each day. Everything was beginning again after lying dormant all winter.

Randy felt as if he, too, had been lying dormant and it was time for him to blossom, to begin again.

Randy was in deep thought as the early morning sun rays streamed through the trees surrounding the house. He had come a long way in only six years, but he had had help from so many people. Now he finally realized how much help and support he had received during those years since the accident.

In some ways the years seemed only like months. But in other ways it seemed like a lifetime, almost as if it had happened to two different people. One who lived before the accident and another who came after. It was as if he had been a fun-loving child before the accident and an adult afterwards.

It was hard to even recall exactly how he had felt right after the accident and during the years of rehabilitation. But he remembered the people who had supported and cared for him through the whole ordeal. Without them and the Lord's saving grace, he would have never made it.

He recalled the months when his mother and grandfather never left his bedside, when Pa's optimism and constant encouragement had kept him from total despair. He thought of his brother, James, always there to assist and comfort him. And his son, Brett, who had been his constant companion the past six years. His entire family had put their lives on hold to support and care for him. Without their love and support, he couldn't have made it.

He had been blessed with supportive, caring friends. He thought about Gary Mitchell often, and they still stayed in contact. There were so many who had been an integral part of his rehabilitation, each providing assistance and support in his or her own way.

His thoughts came back to more recent events. The Super Bull tour was still very fresh on his mind.

The tour had been good for him. In a way, it had been the final step in his rehabilitation. He had no fear of crowds any more and he could wheel himself through the shopping malls with the finesse of a seasoned shopper.

If someone stared at him, it didn't bother him any more. He knew it was the problem of the person who was doing the staring, not him.

He could get in and out of his truck and drive himself wherever he wanted, load and unload his wheelchair, plow his fields with a tractor, ride horses and rope steers, go out to eat in public restaurants, and shop wherever he wanted. He now knew he could do just about anything anyone else could do, and it was a good feeling.

There were many experiences associated with the tour that had given him the opportunity to meet all kinds of people. Many he had met and talked with were people who had visited his booth and wanted to talk about their disabilities. Some had been angry and argumentative, while others had been pleasant and positive.

He remembered the time at Abilene, Texas, where he had met the parents of a young man. They were concerned about their son, who wouldn't respond to therapy and grew more and more bitter and withdrawn each day.

They had heard about Randy and attended the Friday night performance. After talking with Randy, they had asked if Randy would talk with their son if they brought him the next night.

"Yes, ma'am, I'll talk with him. But from what you say, he's in the denial stage. That's a hard time to live through. I know from personal experience. You don't want to hear anything anyone has to say. You're mad at everyone and everything. It's a bad time. And he'll have to want to get on with his life before anyone can help him. He has to want to move on," Randy explained. "Don't expect a few words from anyone to change his attitude, is all I'm saying."

The next night the concerned parents walked up to the National Paralysis Foundation booth pushing their sullen son. He had the familiar angry look that most newly paralyzed persons have. Some soon overcome the feelings of anger, frustration, and fear, but some never do.

Randy attempted to share how he had felt in the beginning—the anger, fears, the feeling of despair, and the disappointments. But, he told the young man, with determination and faith there is always hope.

He had come to terms with his disability and found ways to not only function but participate in the things he enjoyed before the accident. "Everything in this life," he told him, "is give and take regardless of whether a person has a disability or not. Sometimes it's just a little more difficult when you have a disability. That's when you have to try harder."

The young man was just as Randy suspected. He was angry with the world, in complete denial, and he was especially angry toward anyone without a disability. Since he was paralyzed, everyone else should be, too. He wasn't looking for encouragement or assistance in overcoming the paralysis—he was looking for a cure.

Maybe in time the young man would accept the challenge and be able to function again, Randy thought. If not he would remain a bitter, angry man, a person without a future.

There were others that Randy talked with, where he felt as if he had made a difference. And for those he gave special thanks. He simply prayed for the ones like the young man at Abilene.

It was hard at times. But it was as good a therapy for Randy as it was for the people he talked with. In talking with others,

Randy had to face things he had earlier refused to confront.

More than anything, he tried to give the people he talked with encouragement to believe that they could and would overcome the difficult circumstances.

He remembered two brothers, J. W. and Cody Hart, whose parents operate the livestock commission in Gainesville, Texas. Their mother and father accompanied the boys wherever they rodeoed, so Randy and the family became friends. J. W. was sixteen, Cody thirteen.

Mrs. Hart kept a log on each bull and knew the way they bucked and spun. This way J. W. and Cody knew in advance what each bull habitually did and could prepare mentally for their ride.

In Little Rock, Arkansas, Cody had drawn a bull renowned for his treacherous bucking traits. This particular bull had hurt several riders by going into a spin right outside the chutes, then sucking back. By doing this, he would get the cowboy too far forward. Then he would reverse his spin and throw the cowboy to the ground.

If the cowboy was lucky, he was thrown clear, but more often, he was thrown down in front of the bull and either stepped on or butted.

Mrs. Hart told Cody about the bull and the way he bucked, so Cody was prepared. Cody mentally went over and over the upcoming bull ride and by the time it was his turn he knew exactly what he had to do.

When it was Cody's time to ride, Mrs. Hart was standing next to Randy. She was obviously concerned and said so to Randy.

"Mrs. Hart, both J. W. and Cody know how to ride a bull. Cody will be all right," Randy said, smiling.

He tried to make her feel better, but he was concerned himself. Cody couldn't weigh 120 pounds and the bull he was going to ride weighed at least eighteen hundred pounds.

Randy watched as Cody eased down on the bull with help from J. W. and other cowboys who were pulling the rope tight on the bull. Cody nodded his head and the gate flew open.

True to previous performances, the bull came out spinning, then he sucked back. But Cody was ready for him. He sat up on the bull's back like a tick on a dog. But then it was as if he had concentrated on the suck-back move so much that he lost his concentration on the rest of the ride.

The bull got Cody off to the side, then spun away from him. Cody hit the ground hard but was quickly on his feet and running away from the bull towards the fence.

Mrs. Hart gasped as the bull ran at Cody. Randy stiffened and his throat tightened as the bull quickly narrowed the distance between them. It looked as if Cody could make it to the fence before the bull got to him.

But then Cody looked over his shoulder at the bull and stumbled. The bull was almost on top of him when Ronald McDonald, one of the bull-fighting clowns, ran between the bull and Cody. The bull changed direction and darted after Ronald, hooking him high into the air.

Scott Young, the other bull-fighting clown, ran in and helped Cody to his feet, pulling and pushing him to the fence. As Scott pushed Cody to safety, the bull hooked Scott, sending him crashing against the steel fence. Scott rebounded and leapt high upon the arena fence and watched as the giant bull bellowed and pawed. Then the bull turned and went back through the gate.

Randy turned to Mrs. Hart.

"I almost got up and ran out there to help Cody," he said, relieved they were all all right.

Mrs. Hart laughed, patted Randy on the shoulder and went to find her son.

In a few minutes, Mrs. Hart, J. W., and Cody came over to Randy.

"Mama told us about what you said about getting up and running. If us getting hooked would help you walk, me and Cody both would gladly take a hookin'."

Randy looked at the two young cowboys as tears filled his eyes.

"I bet you would, too."

"In a minute," Cody and J. W. both said.

At the same performance in Little Rock, Randy was sitting in the stands when it came his time to perform. The announcer began his introduction as one of Randy's cowboy friends carried him to the arena fence. Then two more cowboys lowered him into his wheelchair.

Randy rolled himself out to the middle of the arena and Travis led Watch Joe up to him. The spotlight was on Randy as George and another good friend, Bimbo, helped him into the saddle. Travis put the rubber bands on the stirrups as Randy pulled the belly band tight.

Then, with the spotlight still on him and Watch Joe, Randy cued the sorrel into a wide-open run around the arena as the announcer told Randy's story. After a couple of circles Randy reined Watch Joe to a sliding stop.

The crowd was on its feet and the whooping and hollering mixed with the applause from ten thousand people was deafening. And it didn't stop even after Randy had completed his ride. Randy rode back into the arena and tipped his hat as the crowd went completely wild.

As he rode back through the entrance alley he glanced up at the audience. There were grown men and women wiping their eyes. As he passed the bull-riding cowboys in the aisle, they congratulated him and there were more than a few misty eyes.

For the first time, Randy felt as if they really knew what he was about and why cowboys are a special breed.

He reached down and patted Watch Joe on the shoulder.

"Thanks, old friend. Thanks for everything. You've more than paid me back."

Randy looked up from his daydreaming as Watch Joe walked out of the barn and stood looking at him.

He thought about how he had nursed the horse after it had been shot. And he wondered if that was all part of a divine plan. He had been there for Watch Joe when he needed him. And Watch Joe had been there for him.

He thought again about Marilyn and the children. Just a few years earlier, he would never have thought this would all be possible: a loving wife, three wonderful, healthy children, and a productive life.

At one time the most important goal he had had was to regain his life—the life he had before the accident. Now that life didn't seem quite as important. He has something better: a family who loves and depends on him and the knowledge that, whatever happens, he can face it.

Like the announcer said, Randy Bird is a champion.

Marilyn's Story

I grew up in Dallas, Texas, with two younger sisters, Donna and Shirley, and one younger brother, David. We lived in the same house from the time I was five years old. In fact, my parents still own that house, although they moved to Caddo Mills about ten years ago.

I met Randy in 1989, when I was working at a department store. Randy and I had mutual friends who introduced us. At first, I would just talk to Randy when he came into the store, but in October of 1989, Randy asked me out. He took me to lunch and introduced me to his son, Brett. We had a great time, and, after that, he began to call me more often. I went to see him at some rodeos, and our relationship just developed from there.

I hadn't ever heard of Randy before I met him, although I was then living in Caddo Mills with my parents, Ruth and Gene Fugitt, about four miles from where Randy and I now live. I was a widow, and had two small children, Christina and Matthew. It was a difficult time in my life, and I could not have coped without the help of my family.

Randy is such a sincere, likable person that I felt an instant trust in him when I met him. Since we married, people have asked me whether I worried about him "taking care" of me and the children. But I've always been pretty independent—I've worked since I was seventeen—so that didn't even cross my mind. They've also asked whether I thought long and hard about loving someone with significant physical difficulties. It seems really strange to me to even try to think that way, for several reasons. First, I've never thought of Randy as handicapped; second, Randy is pretty self-sufficient. Apart from all that, I really love him, and that's what counts.

When people ask me what I'll do as we both get older, when the "responsibilities" of being married to Randy will increase, I tell them we're pretty much like everyone else. We think about our lives now, about our children and how to bring them up as good Christian people, and how to be good Christians ourselves. When we do think of old age, we think of sitting in matching rocking chairs, enjoying our front porch.

That's not to say it's all been easy. Since Randy and I married, we've all had to make adjustments—the kids, Randy, and me. Blending two families is never easy. Randy and Brett, as well as my children and I, shared very close relationships, and those relationships had to undergo certain changes. But it's really encouraging to see how we grow stronger as a family every day.

Everyone takes to Randy, and the children were no

exception. Since Matthew was so young when we married, he's never really known any Daddy other than Randy. Christina had some adjusting to do, as did Brett, but the love we all share helps us get through the difficult times.

The fact that we're proud of Randy helps, too. All of the children love to see him roping in the arena, and we know he takes all the precautions he needs to, so we don't really worry about the danger involved. And, of course, Brett's almost always with him when he's riding, helping him into the saddle and doing anything else Randy needs him to, so that's an added comfort.

We're proud that he's developed and is making a saddle that can help people with disabilities, and we're proud that he speaks to groups everywhere. Randy loves to talk with and to people, because he feels he's making a contribution to their lives—and we know he is!

All in all, we're pretty much like any other family. We have our good days and our bad, our joys and our sorrows—and I suspect that's the way it is for most folks.

—Marilyn Bird

Update from Randy

The writing of this book has forced me to recall the events related to my accident and the years of recovery and rehabilitation that followed. Many of those memories are the stuff of which nightmares are made, and are still emotionally painful.

But there are good memories as well. And the good memories are the ones that remain vivid, while the more negative experiences diminish in intensity over the years. However, there are still times when the painful past comes flooding back, and it takes all the positive reinforcement I can muster to keep it from consuming me. These are the times I keep reminding myself of the four rules of my survival: to have faith in God, desire, dedication, and determination.

There were times after the accident when I blamed God for all the suffering. These were followed by a time when I blamed everyone close to me and anyone else unlucky enough to be around me. Finally I came to realize that it was I, and I alone, who had to shoulder the blame–not God, not my loved ones, not able-bodied people, but Randy Bird. I gradually came to understand that I had to be responsible for myself—with God's loving help—and for my actions during the rest of my life.

It would have been easy to give up and wallow in self-pity during the long months of recovery—to forget about my dreams and desires for the future. But, even now, one of the greatest driving forces is how my giving up when things get tough would seem to my children. What kind of an example would that set for them? That's when desire, dedication, and determination become important. A person has to have the desire for accomplishment, and the dedication and determination to see it through. Nothing worthwhile is easy. You have to learn to put forth that extra effort just when you feel you don't have any more in you.

When I think about my physical condition, I keep reminding myself of a child learning to ride a bicycle. No matter how many times the child falls, he keeps trying until he's mastered it; he just has to find his own way to do it. In the same way, a physically challenged person has to find his own way of doing things. This way might differ from the way a nondisabled person would do it, but it works. Before an accident or disease, you have to make it in life standing up. After an incident that takes away your power to walk, you have to learn to make it sitting down. You're the same person you were before; your dreams and plans for the future may still be the same; you just have to readjust the way you reach them.

In the United States, someone is disabled from an accident or disease every thirty-seven seconds. Currently, there are forty-three million disabled people in the United States alone. This means that the disabled form one of the fastest growing populations in the nation.

While it is not perfect, I believe that the passage this year of the American Disabilities Act allows more opportunities for the disabled to compete in the workplace and to provide a more rewarding lifestyle for themselves and their loved ones.

Pa has always said, "Life's great if you can stand it." So now I have to change the way I stand it. I have to look at life as I now know it, as a new adventure. My life before the accident was a learning experience. My life after the accident is another, altogether different, experience and adventure.

"Experience counts in everything" is another of Pa's sayings. I never really knew exactly what it meant before, but now I do. At the beginning of my adventure after paralysis, I felt conspicuous and uncertain. Each new experience—no matter how physically or mentally painful—was always less challenging and less traumatic than the one before. All of our accomplishments, no matter how challenging, build our confidence and add to our store of experience. This enables us to have the confidence to raise our expectations to yet another level, thereby explaining Pa's saying.

If this book does anything, I hope it will give people encouragement to follow their dreams—and the determination to make them happen. There is always hope, no matter how grim things seem. Don't abandon your plans for the future. Go for it!! You'll find there are people out there willing to help. And God is always there. Look to Him. Your answer is only a prayer away.

God bless you all.

—Randy Bird

Epilogue

I didn't know Randy Bird before his paralyzing accident.
I might have seen him around at rodeos, but he would have
probably just blended in with the rest of the young, huskily
built, self-confident cowboys.

The first time I met Randy he was thin-faced and appeared
small and unassuming, sitting in his wheelchair at a
Greenville, Texas, shopping mall. He had the look and
manner of a cowboy, but the large, wide-brimmed black hat
he was wearing made him look even smaller and his face
thinner.

I had met his brother, James, a few weeks earlier and he
had told me about Randy attempting to produce a special
saddle that would give him enough support to allow him to
ride again.

That seemed impossible to me at the time. And then
when James told me Randy not only planned on riding a
horse again but he was going to compete in team roping, I
thought maybe the accident had done more damage than
his loss of the use of his legs.

Here was a man who looked as if he didn't have the
strength to wheel himself around the mall. How in the

world did he ever think he would be able to ride a horse?

I made polite conversation with Randy about horses and rodeo, then excused myself by telling him I had to go do something or other. I was impressed by his straightforward attitude, and he certainly sounded like he was earnest about riding again, but I couldn't see that happening. As I walked away, I couldn't help feeling sorry for him.

Here was a young man who had his whole life ahead of him just to have it snatched away, or at least it seemed that way to me. I couldn't help but give silent thanks that it wasn't me sitting there kidding myself about trying to ride again.

At that time Randy had already modified a regular western riding saddle and taken a few short rides with James helping him hold on, but that was a long way from actually riding a horse, and light-years away from roping a steer.

It takes a fast, hard-driving roping horse to reach speeds of up to thirty-five or forty miles per hour from a standstill in less than fifty feet when in pursuit of a fast-running steer. It takes horsemanship, balance and strength to not only ride the horse, but to be able to twirl his rope over his head and make a throw at the steer in seconds.

It's not something you can visualize a paralyzed person doing. Matter of fact, there's lots of excellent horse riders who can't handle the speed or don't possess the agility and strength required to be a roper. So to me, it was hard to believe that Randy could ever rope, no matter how much desire he had or what kind of a saddle he invented.

The next time I saw Randy he was working at a western store in the mall. He had built his first saddle, and he and James were practicing roping and going to a few local jackpot ropings. I was impressed beyond belief.

Randy was lifting weights, building muscle, and gaining weight. His hat didn't look quite as big and his voice was even stronger-sounding.

Over the next few months I saw them roping at local jackpots and was amazed at how well Randy and James were performing. I noticed that the other ropers accepted Randy as just another competing cowboy, just someone else they had to beat to win. Randy was not given any edge, nor did he give anyone else any edge. When he rode into a roping arena, he was there to win.

I have watched Randy the past few years as he has healed and matured, and it has been an amazing transformation. In the beginning he pushed himself and everyone around him in his quest to realize what seemed like impossible goals.

Now, he has accomplished what some people would be satisfied to have done in a lifetime.

But to Randy, as soon as a task is accomplished, it's time to move on to the next one.

We get together for team roping practice sessions periodically and Randy never fails to amaze me with his upbeat attitude and his durability. He is always the last one ready to quit. When everyone else is ready to call it a day, Randy is still wanting to rope "just one more."

He keeps everyone entertained with his one-liners and witty remarks and is the first one there to offer sincere advice or assistance to someone just learning how to rope.

There are many things to say about Randy Bird—about all of his accomplishments, his desire to overcome impossible odds, uncommon determination, faith, compassion and perseverance. But I have seen Randy Bird the husband and father, and in my judgment, that outweighs all of the dynamic descriptions.

I've seen and heard Christina shout encouragement to her daddy when he's roping, and Randy smiling proudly back. I've watched as Randy and Brett talked quietly with obvious mutual respect and it's easy to see the unique relationship they share. Then there are the times at the end of a roping session where Marilyn lifts Matthew into the saddle in front of Randy and he rides him around until Matthew is ready to quit.

Maybe it's the suffering, pain, and uncertainty that Randy has endured that makes him what he is now. But whatever it is, there are lots of people in this world who could use a double helping of it.

Glossary

Cantle: The upward-curving rear part of a saddle.

Concho: Ornament that holds the leather to the saddletree.

Dally: To take the loose end of a rope and make at least one, and usually two, complete wraps around the saddle horn.

Girth: A band placed around the belly of a horse for holding a saddle or pack.

Latigo catch: Holds end of latigo, which fastens the girth.

Latigo: Strip of leather, approximately six feet long, which is connected to the drop rig D-ring, and which connects and tightens the girth.

Saddletree: The frame of a saddle.

Springtime Is Coming
By Millicent Collinsworth and Jan Winebrenner
This moving story recounts the life—shadowed by her father's
manic depression, by sexual abuse, and finally by blindness—of
actress Millicent Collinsworth.

New Horizons
By Harry Cordellos and Janet Wells
Harry Cordellos is blind—and a champion athlete! His story is one of
conquering fear and insecurities, of overcoming stereotypes and limitations.

Athletes vs. Cancer
By Robert Brody
Outstanding athletes who have survived cancer are profiled in
this book, which examines the advantages of the athlete's personality
in fighting cancer.

Age of Fear
By William Langlois and John D. O'Connor
San Francisco police officer Bill Langlois was concerned about crimes
against the elderly. He and a special undercover unit set out to do something
about it. *Age of Fear* is a gripping account of his actions and the program he
developed to help the elderly protect themselves.

Standing Tall
By Tucker Church and Paul Harasim
Tucker Church wanted to play Little League baseball, even though he had
cerebral palsy. However, people objected to his having been allowed to
play on a team with younger boys. This is an account of his struggles
and of the operation that allowed him to stand upright.

WRS
PUBLISHING

A Division of WRS Group, Inc.
Waco, Texas